Acknowledgements

"How did the ancient writers of the Bible over 5000 years ago know that the universe had a beginning, whereas it was not until A.D. 1929 that scientists became aware of this and now consider it to be fact? Before this, the scientific consensus was that the universe had always existed. The science of geology is barely 300 years old. It is the study of the rocks of the Earth and the record of events as displayed by the layers deposited over time and the progression of living forms as shown by the fossils that are contained in the rocks, the sequence in which they are displayed is also correctly described in the Bible. Don Daae has made a remarkable achievement in establishing the degree to which the science of geology conforms to God's word. His volumes "Bridging The Gap—Volumes 1 and 2" will answer many questions about the history of the Earth and man's place in it."

Michael Berisoff, P. Geol.

"For Bible readers who wonder how the Biblical story of creation may relate to the geological history of our Earth, this book will provide the answer. Don Daae is an experienced geologist and teacher. He shows that the Genesis record of Creation agrees completely with the geological record. Herein is a valuable addition to the limited number of works that clearly show that the Day Age concept of Creation is both possible and trustworthy."

Mertie Beatty, M.Ed

BRIDGING
THE
GAP

THE FIRST 6 DAYS

REVISED EDITION

OUR PHENOMENAL EARTH – VOL. 1

THE GEOLOGICAL HISTORY OF THE EARTH

H. DONALD DAAE P.GEOL.

WESTBOW
P R E S S
A DIVISION OF THOMAS NELSON

WestBow Press books may be ordered through
booksellers or by contacting:

WestBow Press
A Division of Thomas Nelson
1663 Liberty Drive
Bloomington, IN 47403
www.westbowpress.com
1-(866) 928-1240

ISBN: 978-1-4497-4815-9 (sc)
ISBN: 978-1-4497-4814-2 (hc)
ISBN: 978-1-4497-4816-6 (e)
Library of Congress Control Number: 2012906727
Printed in the United States of America

WestBow Press rev. date: 08/27/2012

Back Cover
Don Daae, P.Geol.

The Biblical references are primarily from the New International
Version and the New King James Version unless otherwise specified.

Many of the figures were originally prepared and drawn by Don
Daae. Many of these figures were then redrawn, assembled
and lettered by Elaine Daae and by Bette Davies.

This manuscript has capitalized all references to the Earth in view
of the fact that it is a proper noun describing a real geographic
place. It is in the same category as other proper nouns like Canada,
Calgary, London, Jerusalem, Paris or Rome. However, Earth is not
capitalized when quoted in the NIV, NKJV or other Bible references.

Table of Contents

Preface xiii
Introduction xv
Foreword xvii

Chapter 1: The First Day of Creation 1
Chapter 2: The Second Day of Creation 78
Chapter 3: The Third Day of Creation 96
Chapter 4: The Fourth Day of Creation. 119
Chapter 5: The Fifth Day of Creation 136
Chapter 6: The Sixth Day of Creation 163

APPENDICIES

APPENDIX A: The Biblical God of Creation 197
APPENDIX B: Yom: The Earth's Long Days 201
APPENDIX C: The Evening and the Morning 205
APPENDIX D: Words For God's Creative Acts. 207
APPENDIX E: Other Creation Concepts. 216
APPENDIX F: Dating the Universe & the Earth 222
APPENDIX G: The Three Heavens 236

List of Figures

Introduction: Figure 1-1:   The History of the Earth. . xviii

Chapter 1:   Figure 1-2:   The First Day of Creation . . . 1

Figure 1-3:   Elohim: The Biblical
Triune God 4

Figure 1-4:   The Biblical Three
Heavens 7

Figure 1-5:   Time When God Laid
the Earth's Cornerstone
and Foundations 13

Figure 1-6:   An Illustration of
Earth's Cornerstone,
Foundations and House. . . . 14

Figure 1-7:   The Geological Record of
the First Day 16

Figure 1-8:   The Magnificent First
Garden of Eden 18

Figure 1-9:   The Day & Night
Cycle Began at the
Commencement of the
Proterozoic Age 33

Figure 1-10: The Birth of the Oceans . . . 36

Figure 1-11: The Proterozoic &
Cambrian Sediments 39

Figure 1-12: The Cambrian Explosion
of Animal Life Illustrated . . . 43

Figure 1-13: A Taxonomy Chart 45

Figure 1-14: The Burgess Shale &
the Cambrian Geology
Illustrated 55

Figure 1-15: The Four Hebrew Words . . . 71

Chapter 2:   Figure 2-1:   The Second Creation
Day 78

Figure 2-2: The Ordovician & Lower & Middle Silurian Illustrated 82

Figure 2-3: Sediments of 2nd Day are Illustrated 90

Chapter 3: Figure 3-1: The Third Creation Day 96

Figure 3-2: Plate Tectonics of 1st & 2nd Days 104

Figure 3-3: Sediments of 3rd Day in Alberta Canada are Illustrated 106

Figure 3-4: 3rd Day Plant & Animal Life are Illustrated 109

Chapter 4: Figure 4-1: The Fourth Creation Day . . 119

Figure 4-2: First Seasonal Rings in Trees 124

Figure 4-3: Plate Tectonics of the 4th Day. 126

Figure 4-4: 4th Day Plant & Animal Life are Illustrated 130

Chapter 5: Figure 5-1: The Fifth Creation Day . . . 137

Figure 5-2: Apatosaurus, a Jurassic Sauropod 146

Figure 5-3: Mosasaurs attacked by pterosaurs. 149

Figure 5-4: 5th Day Plant & Animal Life are Illustrated 150

Chapter 6: Figure 6-1: The Sixth Creation Day . . . 163

Figure 6-2: The 15 Major Orders of Mammals 172

Figure 6-3: A Lower Eocene Amplypod 175

Figure 6-4: A Pleistocene Woolly Mammoth 177

Figure 6-5: The Pleistocene & Recent Age 186

Figure 6-6: Early Man 191

This book is dedicated to my loving wife Evelyn, and to my two daughters Elaine and Connie and to their family members.

Special Thanks

I would like to express my gratitude to Mr. W. Gerry Loewen, B.A., LL B., a personal friend, and to the Rev Lowell L. Young, who under the Lord's guidance were instrumental in giving birth to these series of lectures on Geology, Archaeology and the Bible at the First Alliance Church of the Christian and Missionary Alliance at Calgary, Alberta, Canada in November of 1970.

Special thanks are due to Paul Davies who performed the major edit of the original copy of my first book[2], "Bridging the Gap: The First 6 Days." It was through his commercial art business where he completed the type setting and artwork for my original book, "Bridging the Gap: The First 6 Days." This book became a reality in 1989. It was originally published through Genesis International Research Association in Calgary, Alberta and printed by Spring Arbor Distributors, Belleville, Michigan.

This revised edition of "Bridging the Gap: The First 6 Days, Vol. One." is an updated version of the original 1989 copy. It reveals the remarkable compatibility that exists between the record of geology and the record of the Bible going back in time from the end of the Pleistocene Ice Age to when the crystalline crust of the Earth began to form at about 4.6+ billion years ago.

Many thanks are due to my wife Evelyn for her considerable help and encouragement she has given to me and to my daughter Elaine who assisted with the artwork of many of the Figures.

I wish to thank our Genesis International Research Association Board Members for their encouragements. Many thanks are due to our Chairman Mike Gilders, P.Geol. He assisted with certain figures and with portions of the manuscript. He also originally established our website. I also want to thank Warren Clendining, P.Geol. He set up our present website. See our website at www.gira.ca.

Many thanks are due to our Board Members Mertie Beatty for editing the entire manuscript and to Mike Berisoff, P.Geol. who edited major portions of the manuscript.

Preface

I wish to clarify my personal convictions as a creationist. I am dedicated to the following basic concepts: 1) Special Creation. 2) A literal Bible interpretation. 3) Divine design and purpose in nature. 4) The creation of the Earth about 4.6+ billion years ago. 5) The creation of Man and Woman within the last 10,000 years.

I owe a great debt to the late Walter J. Beasley,[2] F.R.G.S., Past President of the Australian Institute of Archaeology, Melbourne, Australia, whose book *"Creation's Amazing Architect"* has been a major inspiration to me. It was Mr. Beasley who came forward with a chart showing the unique relationship of geology to the six days of creation. This book is an enlargement upon his excellent work. The *History of the Earth* chart included herein is modeled and revised after that of Mr. Beasley. See Figure 1-1.

References

1. H. Donald Daae, P.Geol., *"Bridging the Gap: The First 6 Days." Published* by Genesis International Research Association, Calgary, Alberta. 1989. Printed by Spring Arbor Distributors, Belleville, Michigan.
2. Beasley Walter, F.R.G.S., "AMAZING ARCHITECT," Marshall, Morgan, & Scott, Ltd., London & Edinburgh, 1955

Introduction

The purpose of this revised book is to demonstrate that the science of geology supports and promotes the theological concept of Special Creation. A second purpose is to provide a clarification of the Special Creation position with regard to the Day Age concept, showing how the Biblical Six Days of Creation relate directly to the Geological History of the Earth.

This Day Age concept considers each creation day to be a long period of time, perhaps many millions of years, and that each creation day relates to a certain period of geological time, as outlined in Figure 1-1. This is in contrast to those who believe in the Young Earth Concept, which generally states that the Earth is some 6,000+ years old, and that each day of creation represents a 24-hour day period.

This Day Age concept differs somewhat from the Gap Creationist concept which envisages two separate creations separated by an indefinite period when the Earth was in a waste and void state.

In this book, an appeal is made to the professional earth scientist, lay person, evolutionist, and creationist, to set aside any preconceptions and prejudices, and to consider a new approach to the creation model.

Both the creationist and the evolutionist attempt to explain the origin of the universe, the Earth, plant and animal life and man. They both utilize the same scientific data base in order to construct their models; however their basic philosophies and interpretations are quite divergent.

The details, both scientific and theological of creation and subsequent processes of change influencing our Earth are the subject and discourse of this book.

Figure 1-1, reveals the amazing compatibility that exists between the record of the Bible and the record of Geology. One begins to realize that one can trust both records. The big question arises, how is it possible to trust both records when there appear to be so many diverse opinions? To the Darwinists, this is impossible. To those who believe in Creation Science, this is impossible.

Foreword

by
Pastor Lowell L. Young
Calgary, Alberta, 1988

The Author of this much needed volume, Mr. Donald Daae, is fully qualified to write from both a spiritual and professional standpoint. Spiritually, he knows the Bible. Professionally, he knows geology.

These chapters were born in the womb of teaching. As Mr. Daae's Pastor, I had the privilege of giving birth to the lessons in our adult Elective Studies. Soon, the knowledge of the series was area-wide. Demand for the course was great.

Mr. Daae now writes to me and graciously invites me to append my words of introduction. Those who have listened and learned from these lectures, as well as those who have not heard by the hearing of the ear, will profit from this permanent form.

I embrace with elation the privilege of commending this book and invite you, in the words of Tennyson's appeal of nature.

> Come walk with me, she said,
> Into realms yet untrod,
> And read what still is unsaid
> In the manuscripts of God.

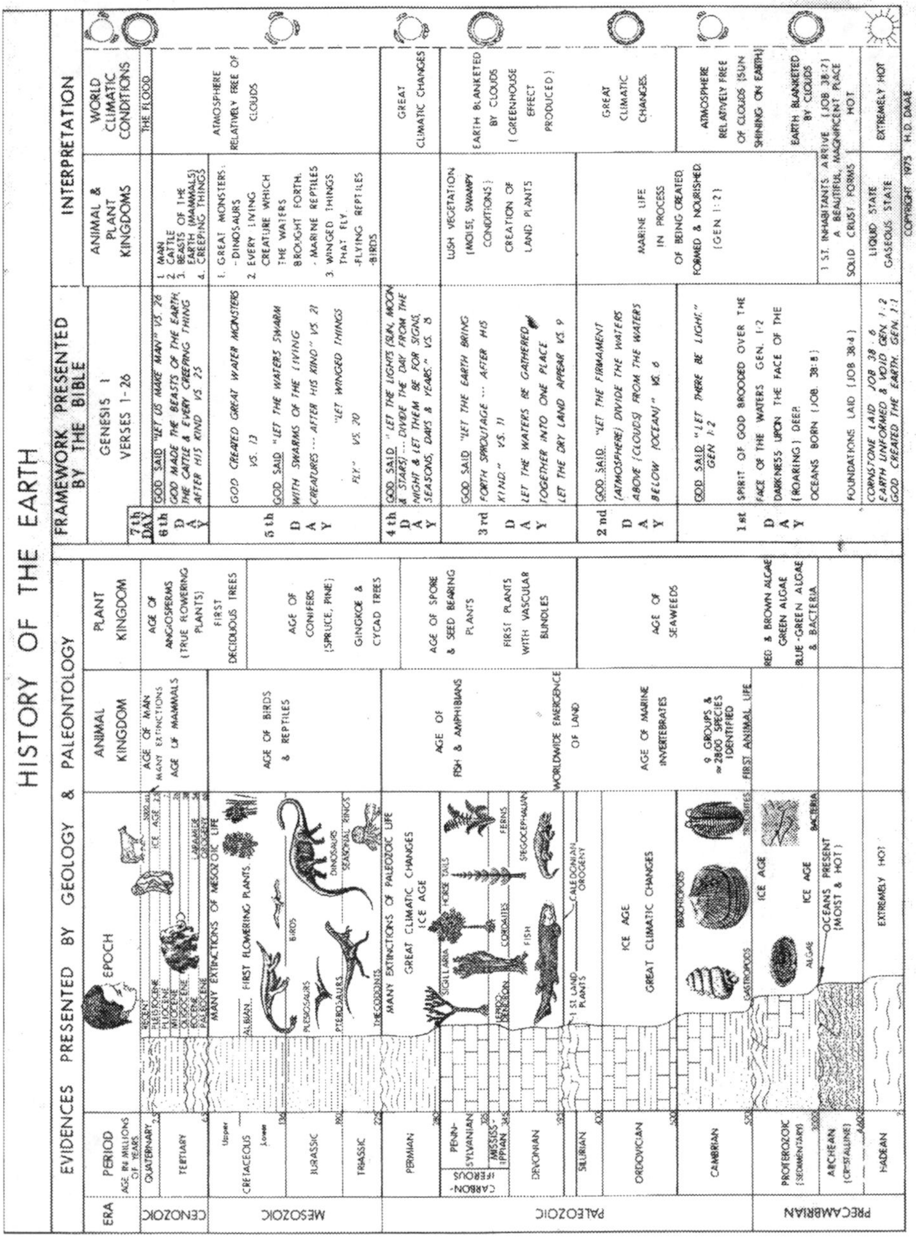

HISTORY OF THE EARTH

Figure 1-1: History of the Earth as it relates to the Record of Geology and to the Record of the Bible.

Chapter 1

The First Day of Creation

Introduction

The First Day of Creation began the moment God began his work of old. The Bible alludes to this moment and to the period of time prior to the First Day as follows:

"The Lord possessed me (wisdom) in the beginning of his way, BEFORE HIS WORKS OF OLD. I was set up from everlasting, from the beginning before the earth was." (Proverbs 8:22-23, NKJV).

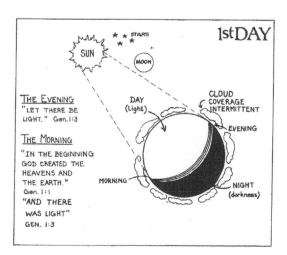

Figure 1-2: The First Day of Creation.
It reveals what the Earth was like towards the latter part of the First Creation Day.

The time that existed prior to the creation of the universe, the heavens and the Earth is infinite. God has always been. He is from everlasting to everlasting as is recorded in the following passage:

"Before the mountains were brought forth, or ever You had formed the earth and the world, even from everlasting to everlasting, You are God." Psalm 90:2, (NKJV).

The question arises where did God reside prior to the creation of the universe and the Earth? The answer to this profound question would be simply this: **God has always resided in His Third Heaven**. This is God's Home. This is where He resides today and is where He has always resided in ages past. It is in a different dimension that is presently in the realm of the invisible. It is also the future home of all believers who have been willing to allow the Triune God to take up residency into their own heart and life.

Figure 1-2 reveals what the Earth was like after the Fall of Lucifer and at the very beginning of the Proterozoic Age. See Figure 1-1. However, what was the Earth like prior to this time? Geologists state that the oldest rocks on Earth and samples brought back from the moon, based upon radiometric methods of dating, would be about 4.6+ billion years in age. This would mean that God began His work of old was even of an earlier age. See Figure 1-1.

In this Chapter we will examine the different historical and geological stages that the Earth has experienced during the First Day of Creation. In order to do this, we will now begin to open the window pertaining to the Biblical and the Geological history of the First Day of Creation. But first, let us gain a brief insight into who is God?

Who is God?

Our finite minds demand a beginning and an end, but with God there is no beginning and no end. God is the great timeless One as He stated to Moses in Exodus 3:14 (NKJV), "I AM WHO I AM." God is always in the eternal present as the great "I AM" of the universe. **He is also the High and Lofty One who inhabits eternity.** We read in Isaiah 57:15 (NKJV), *"For thus says the High and Lofty one who inhabits eternity, whose name is Holy:" I dwell in the high and holy place, with him who has a contrite and humble spirit, to revive the spirit of the humble, And to revive the heart of the contrite ones."* He is the all powerful, all knowing and everywhere present God, who is the same yesterday, today, and forever. He is the great unchanging God. We will change and all creation will change, but God will always be the same throughout all time and eternity.

God revealed to Moses that He has always been when He said, *"I Am that I Am"* (Exodus 3:14). God is always in the eternal present, as the great "I AM" of the universe.

God the Father can be likened to the Great Divine Architect. He is the one who came forth with an architectural plan, blueprint and design for the universe of stars and galaxies and the Earth. God the Son can be likened to the Great Divine Creator and Carpenter. He is the one who created this vast universe of stars and galaxies and the Earth according a plan set out by His Heavenly Father. God the Holy Spirit can be likened to the Great Divine Indweller. He is the one who indwells all space and time. In other words, God the Father, God the Son and God the God Holy Spirit were co-workers in the overall work of planning, creating, forming, sustaining and indwelling the heavens and the Earth. See Figure 1-3.

Figure 1-3: Elohim, the Biblical Triune God.

How Big is God?

God has to be bigger than the universe of stars and galaxies. The God of the Bible has three distinct qualities. He is Omnipresent, Omniscient and Omnipotent.

According to Webster's College Dictionary[1], "*Omnipresent means being present everywhere at the same time.*" King David in 2 Kings 2:5-6 (NIV) summed it up neatly when he said, "*The temple I am going to build will be great, because our God is greater than all other gods. 6But who is able to build a temple for him, since the heavens, even the highest heavens, cannot contain him?*" This means that the vast universe of stars and galaxies is too small to contain the God of the Bible. See Figure 1-3.

However, God's Highest Heaven refers to God's Third Heaven which extends far beyond our universe of stars and galaxies into infinity. It is presently in the realm of the invisible. This means that God's Third Heaven is presently in a different dimension to that of the Earth and the universe.

According to Webster's Dictionary, Omniscient means, "*Having complete or unlimited knowledge.*" It refers to God's ability to know absolutely everything. The Apostle Paul says, "*Nothing in all creation is hidden from God's sight. Everything is uncovered and laid bare before the eyes of him to whom we must give account.*" (Hebrews 4:13, NIV). Truly God is the source of all knowledge. This gives a glimpse into the unlimited, infinite greatness of God. All knowing means there is nothing that God does not know.

God is Omnipotent. This means He has infinite and unlimited power. God spoke the entire universe of stars and galaxies into existence. We read in Genesis 1:1 (NIV) "*In the beginning God created the heavens and the earth.*" The magnitude of this accomplishment has only been realized during recent times through the science of astronomy. We indeed serve an awesome God.

The Triune God

The God of the Bible is a Triune God. The Hebrew word for the Triune God is **"Elohim.**" It is a masculine Hebrew noun that is always in the plural. It signifies a three in one relationship, God the Father, God the Son and God the Holy Spirit. We read in Genesis 1:26 where God (Elohim) says, "*Let **us** make man in **our** image, after **our** likeness.*" In this brief sentence, the plurality of the Godhead is brought out three times.

According to the Bible, God is infinite and the time prior to the creation of the universe and the Earth is infinite. God has always been. He is from everlasting to everlasting as is recorded in Psalm 90:2 (NKJV), "*Before the mountains were brought forth, or ever you had formed the earth and the world, even from everlasting to everlasting, you are God.*" How long is everlasting?

Our finite minds demand a beginning and an end, but with God there is no beginning and no end. God is the great timeless One, as He stated to Moses, "I AM WHO I AM" (Exodus 3:14 NKJV). God is always in the eternal present, as the great "I AM" of the universe. He is the High and Lofty One who inhabits all eternity. He is the all powerful, all knowing, everywhere present God. He is the supreme intelligence behind all Creation. He never changes. He is the same yesterday, today and forever (Hebrews 13:8).

There is no beginning or end with God. However, when it comes to all that He has created and made within the universe of stars and galaxies, then the following verse applies, *"I am the Alpha and Omega, the beginning and the end, says the Lord."* (Revelations 1:8, NKJV). He is the one who has brought all visible things within the universe into being and He will also bring about their demise. This verse only applies to the visible world that belongs to the Biblical First and second Heavens. From the vantage point of man standing on the Earth, the First Heaven is the Earth. The Second Heaven is the universe of stars and galaxies. The Third Heaven is God's Home.

God's Three Heavens

The Bible describes God's three heavens. In Genesis 1:1, we read, *"In the beginning God created the heavens and the earth."* In this verse the heavens relate to the universe of stars and galaxies that extends into space for multi trillions of earth miles and it is referred to as God's **Second Heaven**. The Earth together with its surrounding firmament is referred to as **God's First Heaven** because it is very much alive. We read in Genesis1:8 NKJV, *"and God called the firmament heaven."*

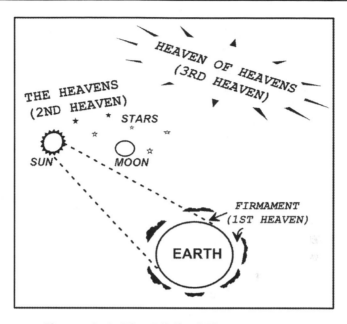

Figure 1-4: The Biblical Three Heavens

The Third Heaven is God's Home and it is in a different dimension. It is presently in a dimension that is invisible to us. This is where God dwells. This is also the future home of all believers. Paul says in 2 Corinthians 12:2-10, "*2 I know a man in Christ who fourteen years ago was caught up to **the third heaven**. Whether it was in the body or out of the body I do not know—God knows. 3And I know that this man—whether in the body or apart from the body I do not know, but God knows—4was caught up to paradise and heard inexpressible things, things that no one is permitted to tell. 5I will boast about a man like that, but I will not boast about myself, except about my weaknesses. 6Even if I should choose to boast, I would not be a fool, because I would be speaking the truth. But I refrain, so no one will think more of me than is warranted by what I do or say, 7or because of these surpassingly great revelations. Therefore, in order to keep me from becoming conceited, I was given a thorn in my flesh.*" It was on Paul's First Missionary Journey at Lystra that Paul was stoned and then he was dragged out of the city as dead. It is believed that this was the time that

Paul experienced death and was given a brief glimpse into the immense beauty of God's Third Heaven. This also reveals how close we are to God's Third Heaven at all times. It is always only an instant away.

In reality God's Third Heaven encompasses our Earth, the entire universe of stars and galaxies and extends into infinity into all space and time.

The number of Earth years that would represent eternity past is beyond our ability to measure. However, the number of years to the time when God began his work of old and created the first star within the universe of stars and galaxies would be within our number system. God has chosen not to reveal this specific date to us, or the date when he created the Earth, but simply says "*It was in the beginning.*"(Genesis1:1).

Man can speculate as to the age of the universe and the Earth, but they are only educated guesses.

For centuries, man has attempted to explain the origin of the Earth by both scientific and religious hypotheses. Endeavors in the pure sciences have attempted to describe the origin, or formation, of the Earth on the basis of what can be observed, measured and verified through laboratory experimentation. While this approach is entirely satisfactory in many other instances, it is inadequate to answer the question as to the exact origin and age of the Earth.

There are no first-hand measurements or observations available, as there were, obviously, no men existing at the time. As a result, the scientist is forced to evaluate other evidences together with his or her best available laboratory data. In effect, scientific, philosophical and theological considerations become relevant and necessary to formulate a balanced and sound hypothesis.

Can Long Geological Ages Be Trusted?

Earth scientists have estimated the age of the Earth at about 4.6 billion years. This date is based primarily on geological evidences and the prevailing geological standard for the estimation of transpired time, the fossil record and radiometric aging.

Radiometric aging, or radioactive dating, is a method of estimating the age of a material. The procedure is based on measuring the rate of disintegration of radioactive elements in a given sample of material. By comparing the concentration of radio-isotopes with the concentration of similar stable isotopes, the age of a rock sample can be estimated. Radiometric and other methods of dating are discussed in Appendix F.

I would like to quote Dr. Roger C. Wiens[2] who says, *"Radiometric dating—the process of determining the age of rocks from the decay of their radioactive elements—has been in widespread use for over half a century. There are over forty such techniques, each having a different way of measuring them. It has become increasingly clear that these radiometric dating techniques agree with each other and as a whole, present a coherent picture in which the earth was created a very long time ago. Many Christians are completely unaware of the great number of laboratory measurements that have shown these methods to be consistent, and they are also unaware that Bible-believing Christians are among those actively involved in radioactive dating."*

An alternate interpretation for measuring the age of the Earth is based on Biblical chronology. One such interpretation is based upon the Catastrophic Flood Theory. It indicates the age of the Earth to be some six to eight thousand years old. These people are known as Young Earth Creationists or Creation Science persons. See APPENDIX E.

There are a number of other related, differing, contemporary theories as well. The existence of alternate interpretations of similar data highlights a certain difficulty in combining philosophical and religious ideas with traditional scientific evidences and that of faith.

There are those who hold to the "Day Age Theory". This is the view that is emphasized in this manuscript. It considers each creation day to be a long period of time that could be many millions of Earth years in length. We believe that the record of geology can be trusted. On this basis it is possible to deduce that the Earth came into existence many millions of years ago.

Biblical evidence is rigorous only given the conviction that the scriptures are true and infallible. Even then, differences of opinion can arise as to the precise meaning of a given passage, even between individuals of the same basic religious and scientific convictions.

These are not irresolvable difficulties. As in any discipline, there is a most substantive, or most rigorous, view which tends to diminish the credibility of alternate views. Even so, these questions cannot be posed in terms of right and wrong, rather only the degree to which they concur with the available information, and their resulting rational, logical and spiritual appeal.

The purpose of this chapter is to derive this logical account, or explanation, from scientific information obtained from the geological record and from the record of events as detailed in the Bible. We will be examining the origin of the Earth, the formation of the Earth's interior, its cornerstone and foundations, the sudden appearance of ocean water, the establishment of a sophisticated environment, the origin of life, the sudden advent of plant and animal species in the fossil record, the perpetuity of life and much more.

Bible Record of the First Day

The First Day of Creation is recorded in the Bible in Genesis 1:1-5 (NKJV), as follows, *"In the beginning God created the heavens and the earth. And the earth was without form and void; and darkness was upon the face of the deep. And the Spirit of God moved upon the face of the waters. And God said, Let there be light: and there was light. And God saw the light, that it was good: and God divided the light from the darkness. And God called the light Day, and the darkness he called Night. And the evening and the morning were the first day."* Each phrase and word in this passage is highly significant. See Figure 1-2. See APPENDICIES B & C.

In the Middle East, the new day always began at sunset. It was in the evening that the people would plan what they would do in the morning. The night was a time of rest. At sunrise, early in the morning, they would commence the work necessary to accomplish certain aspects of this plan conceived the evening before. During the day they would complete the plan. Then in the evening they would plan what they would do the next day.

The plan conceived by God the Father, the Great Divine Architect in the evening of the First Day is described in Genesis 1:3: *"And God said, Let there be light."* This is a plan. God envisaged a universe of light. Every star and galaxy in space was to be a source of light or would reflect light. The latter portion of Genesis 1:3 relates to the work being done by the Creator where we read, *"And there was light."* This passage relates to the culmination of the plan for the First Creation Day. The Great Divine Creator and Carpenter performed the work necessary to bring the universe of light into existence during the morning and throughout the First Creation Day. See Figure 1-3.

Geological Record of the First Day

There is truly a remarkable compatibility that exists between the record of Geology and the record of the Bible. We will now begin to investigate these various relationships that exist throughout the long geological history of the Earth's First Day of Creation. See Figure 1-1.

The Hadean Age

The Hadean Age represents a time in the early history of the Earth when it was in an extremely hot gaseous state. Is it possible that God may have originally created the Earth in an extremely hot gaseous or formless state? Is it possible that the early Earth was like a bright star shining in the firmament of the heavens in the beginning? See Figure 1-1.

Is it possible that God through His Son spoke the Earth into existence by the power of His Word much earlier than 4.6 billion years ago? We read in Genesis 1:2a, *"The earth was formless and empty"* (NIV). What does formless and empty mean? For instance, a granite rock has a definite form at normal temperatures. However, if granite is heated to its melting point, it would revert to a liquid. If it is heated to a higher temperature it will revert to an intensely hot gaseous state. If the Earth was in a very hot gaseous state, it would not have had a definite form. In other words every substance on Earth can exist in either a solid, liquid or gaseous state.

The Earth's Cornerstone & Foundations

At the moment of creation, the Earth was obviously created in an extremely hot gaseous or formless state. It was during this early period of time called the Hadean Age that God began to lay the cornerstone and the foundations of the Earth.

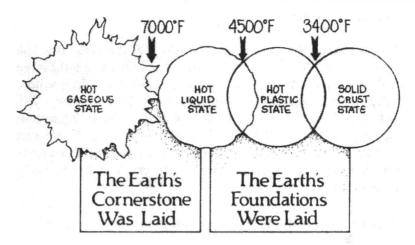

Figure 1-5: Time when God Laid the Earth's Cornerstone and Foundations.

In Job 38: 1-6 (NKJV), God presented Job with a very interesting set of questions saying, "*Where were you when I laid the earth's foundation? Tell me, if you understand. Who marked off its dimensions? Surely you know! Who stretched a measuring line across it? On what were its footings set, or who laid its cornerstone?*"

Walter Beasley[3] and others have described as a process, the following four steps in the geological development of the Earth: a hot gaseous state, a high temperature liquid state, a hot plastic state and a solid crust state. These four stages represent a cooling process. Although the original maximum temperatures of the gases cannot be known, it is known that if the Earth cooled to about 3870°C (7000°F) degrees, it would have begun to revert to a liquid state. At about 2480°C (4500°F) degrees it would have begun to revert to a hot plastic state. At about 1870°C (3400°F) degrees Fahrenheit a thin, solid crystalline crust would have begun to form. In other words, the moment a solid crystalline crust began to form on the early Earth marks the end of the Hadean Age and the beginning of the Archean Age.

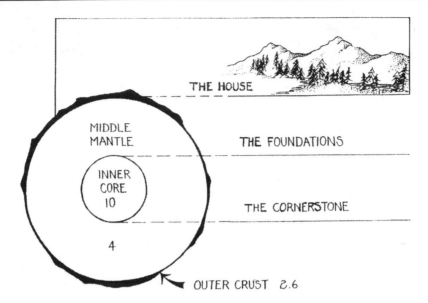

Figure 1-6: An illustration of Earth's Cornerstone, Foundations and House.

The Bible pictures the Earth as a large building having an inner cornerstone, a foundation and an outer crust. Geology illustrates the Earth with an inner core having a density of 10, a foundation with a density of 4, an outer crust with a density of 2.6 and a house where life dwells. See Figure 1-6. The cornerstone and the foundation give stability to the house as the Earth rotates on its axis in an orbit around the sun. What do we mean by the Earth's House? Was the Earth being prepared as a house towards the end of the Hadean Age?

The Archean Age

We may ask the question, what is so significant about the Archean Age? It was a period in the Earth's history that spans about 800+ million years according to the science of geology. See Figures 1-1 and 1-7. According to conventional geology, this age is a mystery. There are no direct evidences of life of any nature to be found in the rocks of this geological age nor are there any direct evidences of ocean water or water laid sediments.

During my third year at university, I had the privilege of spending four months on a geological Field Party on the Great Canadian Precambrian Shield in northern Saskatchewan in the vicinity of the Churchill and the Reindeer River regions. The ancient crystalline rocks of Archean Age are the predominant rocks in all the major Precambrian Shield regions throughout the Earth. About 75% of all these Archean rocks are granite related. These granite type rocks are then intruded by later darker basaltic and andesitic igneous intrusions and volcanic type of rocks. It is obvious that the Archean Age ended with great heat and tectonic activity.

When I was at university, my geological companions and professors often wondered why there was an absence of life on Earth during this long Archean Age. When I was on this geological field party in Northern Saskatchewan we desperately looked for evidences of past life in rocks of the Archean age, but to no avail.

Earth: A Place of Habitation

Life is never found in the cornerstone or the foundation of any building. Life is always found in the house. The Earth was destined to be a place of habitation. The question remains when did the Earth first become inhabited?

Much information has been gained through the geological and geophysical sciences with respect to the complexities and the amazing dynamics of the Earth's interior. Earth scientists have been able to determine the varying thicknesses of the Earth's crust in continental and ocean regions. This gives a basic understanding why the Earth is designed for life and habitation.

When the record of the Bible is related to the record of geology, we soon begin to realize that the Earth has been a place of habitation from the beginning of the Archean Age to the present. See Figures 1-1 and 1-7. How can this be? Who were the Earth's first inhabitants?

In order to understand who the first inhabitants of the Earth were it is important that we gain a better understanding of where they came from? It is thus, important that we gain an insight into God's Three Heavens.

The Geological Column During the The First Day of Creation

Earth's Golden Age |—— Age of New Beginnings ——

Hadean Age	Archean Age		Proterozoic Age	Cambrian Age
4.7 b. yrs	4.6 b.yrs.	3.8 b.yrs.		5.44 -5.10 m.yrs
	1ST Inhabitants Arrive	The Fall of Lucifer	Birth of the Oceans	Explosion
	EARTH A MAGNIFICENT PLACE		SOPHISTICATED FOOD CHAIN ESTABLISHED (Bacteria & Algae)	of
				Animal Life
	1ST Garden of Eden		A Dark Sin Cursed Earth	

Figure 1-7: The Geological Record of the First Day of Creation. The length of the Hadean Age is unknown. The Archean Age is about 800+ million years. The Proterozoic Age is about 3.3 billion years. The Cambrian Age is now estimated to be about 34 million years in length. These dates are based upon radiometric dating methods. See the quote by Dr. Roger C. Wiens.[2] This Figure was drawn by Don Daae and was then computer generated by geologist Mike Gilders. Compare with Figure 1-1.

God's Three Heavens

The concept of heaven is entrenched in our literature, our culture and our thinking. Every person has a deep inner desire to go to heaven, but the question arises, where is heaven located? What is heaven like? How do I get there?

The Bible has much to say about heaven and we are told in Genesis 1:8 that, *"God called the firmament heaven."* Is heaven no greater than the firmament, which is the hydrosphere? Is this the same heaven mentioned in Genesis 1:1 which says, *"In the beginning God created the heavens and the earth."* Could there possibly be more than one heaven? Paul speaks about being taken up to the Third Heaven for we read in 2 Corinthians 12:2, *"God knows, such a one was caught up to the third heaven."* It becomes evident upon analyzing and comparing the various passages of scripture that the Bible is describing three different Heavens (see Figure 1-4).

The Hebrew word for heaven is shomayim. It is a noun that is always in the plural. It is used to describe each of the three heavens. All three heavens reflect the Trinity of God. They are in reality one heaven with three distinct component parts.

The First Heaven

From the vantage point of man standing on the Earth, the First Heaven that one observes is the firmament. Genesis 1:8 says, *"God called the firmament heaven." We read in Psalm 19:1b, "The firmament shows God's handiwork."* When one observes the beautiful mountains, the sweeping prairies, the vast desert areas, the lush, beautiful vegetation of the tropics, one is beholding what the Bible is referring to as the "First Heaven." It is literally teaming with plant and animal life of all descriptions. It is that portion of our Earth that is able to sustain life. It encompasses the oceans with all its aquatic life, and the biosphere where you and I dwell. Every breath of air that we breathe is a gift from the First Heaven. It is a beautiful place that is very much alive. However, this is a description of the Earth today. What could the Earth have been like during the Archean Age?

Figure 1-8: The Magnificent First Garden of Eden. Prepared by Don Daae.

The Second Heaven

The Second Heaven is the physical universe. The very first verse of the Bible says, *"In the beginning God created the heavens and the earth"* (Genesis 1:1). From the vantage point of the Earth looking out into space, all the heavenly bodies including the sun, moon and the trillions of stars and galaxies are included with this heaven. The psalmist briefly describes this heaven, *"When I consider thy heavens, the work of your fingers, the moon and the stars that you have ordained, what is man that You are mindful of him,"* (Psalm 8:3). The Second Heaven includes the millions of galaxies, quasars, pulsars, solar systems, spheres of all descriptions and sizes in this vast area called the universe.

The fact that God is present throughout the universe makes it very much alive. The Bible is very clear that God's holy angels are continually commuting back and forth from the Third Heaven to the Earth and always for a specific purpose. It is also possible that God's holy angelic beings are being delegated by God to various other parts of the universe for specific purposes. For instance when Jesus was born in Bethlehem 2000 years ago, an angel appeared to the Shepherds announcing the good news that a Savior had been born who is Christ the Lord. This was followed by a great company of the heavenly hosts who were praising God and saying, "*Glory to God in the highest, and on earth peace to men on whom His favor rests.*" (Luke 2: 8—14).

The Third Heaven

The Bible describes the Third Heaven as God's home. Paul tells about an experience of having been caught up into the Third Heaven for we read, "*I know a man in Christ who fourteen years ago was caught up to the third heaven.*" (2 Corinthians 12:2) In the context of this chapter, we realize Paul was literally taken up into the Third Heaven. He was taken to paradise. This is where the Heavenly Mount Zion is located. This is where our prayers ascend. This is where God the Son, the Lord Jesus Christ is seated at the right hand of God the Father, continually interceding on our behalf. This is the Mission Control Centre of the universe. God has complete control over the entire universe and over all creation from the Third Heaven. He knows exactly what is taking place at every place at all times.

The Third Heaven is God's home and is very much alive. The Bible gives many references to the beauty and grandeur of this Heaven. In Psalm 48: 1-3 we read, "*Great is the Lord and most worthy of praise, in the city of our God, his holy mountain. It is beautiful in its loftiness, the joy of the whole earth. Like the utmost heights of Zaphon is Mount Zion, the city of the Great King. God is in her citadels.*" Then we read in Hebrews 12:22-24, *"You have come to Mount Zion, to the heavenly Jerusalem, the city of the living God. You have come to thousands of angels in joyful assembly, to the church of the firstborn, whose names are written in heaven. You have come to God, the judge of all men, to the spirits of righteous men made perfect, to Jesus the mediator of the new covenant and to the sprinkled blood that speaks a better word than the blood of Able."*

The only part of reality that is detectable by our five senses is the physical universe and the Earth. We as finite human beings are able to see and observe the First and Second Heavens, but we are unable to see or discern the Third Heaven, because it resides within the realm of the invisible. It is within a different frequency or dimension. According to the Bible, reality consists of both the visible and the invisible for we read, *"For by Him (the Lord Jesus Christ) all things were created that are in heaven and on earth, visible and invisible, whether thrones or rulers or authorities. All things were created by Him and for Him. And He is before all things and in Him all things hold together"* (Colossians 1:16&17, NIV).

The Three Heavens are as One

The Third Heaven, where God dwells, is often referred to as the Highest Heaven or the Heaven of Heavens. We read in Nehemiah 9:6, *"You are the Lord. You made the heavens (second heaven), even the highest heavens, and all their starry host (third heaven), the earth and all things on it, the seas and all that is in them (first heaven), and You give life to everything. The hosts of heaven worship you."* The hosts of heaven refer to all of God's holy angelic beings and to all human beings who have and will receive Jesus Christ as their personal Savior and Lord.

Thus, we see that the First Heaven includes the oceans as well as the Earth with its great variety of life. It becomes apparent that the First and Third Heavens are very much alive. Is it possible that the Second Heaven which includes the vast universe of galaxies may also be very much alive? The omnipresence of the Triune God throughout the entire universe makes it very much alive. It is also highly possible that God's holy angels commute back and forth from the Third Heaven to various parts of the universe as well as to the Earth. We can safely say that all Three Heavens are very much alive.

The Bible acknowledges God as the sole owner of the Three Heavens for we read in Deuteronomy 10:14, "*To the Lord your God belong the heavens (second heaven), the highest heaven (third heaven), the earth and everything in it (first heaven).*" God has total ownership of His creation by the mere fact that He is the Creator of all things. The Bible says, "*For every animal of the forest is mine, and the cattle on a thousand hills. I know every bird in the mountains and the creatures of the field are mine. If I were hungry I would not tell you, for the world is mine, and all that is in it*" (Psalm 50:10-11 NIV). In other words, God owns every species and variety of animal and plant life on the Earth. He has placed man on the Earth to look after and to be a good steward of all that He has made for we read, "*Let us make man in our image, in our likeness, and let them rule over the fish of the sea and the birds of the air, over the livestock, over all the creatures that move along the ground.*" (Genesis 1:26 NIV) See Figure 1-8.

We may stand in awe at the wonders, beauty, and magnificence of God's creation as revealed in the First and Second Heavens. However, this is only a glimpse of a far surpassing beauty, magnificence, vastness, glory and awesomeness of the Third Heaven which is God's home and will also be our future home. If the Third Heaven appears great and glorious, how much greater, more glorious, beautiful, majestic and awesome must God be. Even reason and logic say to us that the Creator must always be greater than what He has created for we read, *"The Lord is high above all nations and His glory is above the Heavens"* (Psalm 113:4).

Earth's First Inhabitants

The Bible states that the primary purpose or reason why God planned, created, formed and made the Earth in the beginning was that **it would be a place of habitation**. We read, *"Thus says the Lord who created the heavens, Who is God who formed the earth and made it, Who has established it, Who did not create it in vain, Who formed it to be inhabited, I am the Lord and there is no other"* (Isaiah 45:18, NKJV). In the beginning, God created the Earth so that its inhabitants would honor and glorify Him. We read in "Isaiah 43:7, NKJV, *"All who claim me as their God will come, for I have made them for my glory. It was I who created them."* We know that man is the present inhabitant on our Earth. This leads to a second question, was man the first inhabitant of our Earth? According to the Bible man was not the first inhabitant, but was the second.

The Bible states very clearly to us that **the first or original inhabitants on this Earth were Lucifer and his angels.** They arrived during the early part of the First Day of Creation. God placed them in a beautiful Garden on Earth called Eden. This first Garden of Eden is not to be confused with Adam and Eve's Garden of Eden. The First Garden called Eden was decked with beautiful gemstones. At this early period of time, the Earth was a most beautiful, magnificent place. It would have appeared like a beautiful, sparkling gemstone from a distance. See Figure 1-8.

It is herein believed that this beautiful and magnificent First Garden of Eden encompassed the entire Earth as there were no oceans present at that time. It was a place where Lucifer and his angels served and worshipped Almighty God for about 800+ million Earth years.

A Joyous Celebration in the Third Heaven

There was great joy, singing and celebration among the cherubim and the angels in the God's Third Heaven because the Earth had just been created and prepared for habitation. God the Father through His Son the Lord Jesus Christ, the Creator of all things, had just prepared this most magnificent place called Eden, the Garden of God on Earth. It was prepared as a most beautiful place of habitation for Lucifer and the angels under his jurisdiction.

This amazing time within the Third Heaven of great jubilation took place after God had laid the Earth's cornerstone and foundations. A brief glimpse into this joyous occasion is recorded in Job 38:4-7 (NKJV) "*4Where were you when I laid the foundation of the earth? Tell me, if you have understanding.5 Who determined its measurements? Surely you know! Or who stretched the line upon it? 6To what were its foundations fastened? Or who laid its cornerstone—7while the morning stars sang together and all the sons of God shouted for joy?*"

We then read about this same joyous occasion in the New International Version as follows, "*4Where were you when I laid the earth's foundation? Tell me, if you understand.5 Who marked off its dimensions? Surely you know! Who stretched a measuring line across it? 6On what were its footings set, or who laid its cornerstone—7while the morning stars sang together and all the angels shouted for joy?*" (Job 38:4-7 NIV) This joyous time of celebration took place within God's Third Heaven just prior to the time when Lucifer and his angels arrived on planet Earth at the very beginning of the Archean Age. Figures 1-7, 1-8 & 1-1.

Two groups of created angelic beings are referred to as follows: the Morning Stars who sang together and all the Sons of God who shouted for joy. The question arises who were the Morning Stars? The clue is to be found in the name

Lucifer which means Morning Star? Isaiah 14:12 informs us that **Lucifer was the Son of the Morning** for we read, "*How are you fallen from heaven, O Lucifer, son of the morning!*" (NKJV) It is believed that Lucifer was one of these Morning Stars that sang together at that time of great jubilation? Since Lucifer was a Cherub, it is believed that the Morning Stars were the Cherubim of Heaven that were singing together and rejoicing that the Most High God of Heaven and Earth had just prepared the Earth as a place of habitation for Lucifer and his angels.

Cherubim are a group of the second highest order of angelic beings in God's Third Heaven. They are described in the Bible as having wings (Exodus 25:20, NKJV). Ezekiel describes the cherubim in Ezekiel 10:19 as follows, "*And the cherubim lifted their wings and mounted up from the earth in my sight.*" In verse 21, we read, "*Each one had four wings and the likeness of the hands of a man under their wings.*" During this period of Earth's history there was great joy, celebration and wonderful harmony among all the angelic beings.

The big question arises, who are the Sons of God who also shouted for joy at the time when the Earth had just been prepared for habitation? Bible scholars generally agree that they were the multi millions of angels in God's Third Heaven. They were filled with joy and gladness because God had now prepared the Earth as a place of habitation for them as well. See Figure 1-8.

Who Was Lucifer?

Lucifer was a being of great beauty as the scripture relates, "*You were the seal of perfection, full of wisdom and perfect in beauty*" (Ezekiel 28:12b, NKJV). This verse reflects the inner beauty and character of Lucifer when he was created. "*You were blameless in your ways from the day you were created till wickedness was found in you."* Ezekiel 28:13-15 (NIV)

Lucifer was a guardian cherub upon God's Holy Mount Zion in God's Third Heaven. We read in Ezekiel 28:14, *"You were anointed as a guardian cherub, for so I ordained you. You were on the holy mount of God."* The Holy Mountain of God is located on Mount Zion within God's Third Heaven. Lucifer was one of the many Cherubim in God's Heaven. The fact that Lucifer was anointed by God as a guardian cherub may indicate that he may have been chief among the other Cherubim. He certainly was chief among all the other angelic beings on Earth.

Ezekiel 28:13b, (NKJV) says of Lucifer, *"The workmanship of your timbrels and pipes were prepared for you on the day that you were created."* This verse implies that Lucifer was created with musical abilities.

The First Garden of Eden

In the beginning, God in His great love created and formed the Earth in a most detailed and magnificent manner in preparation for its first inhabitants. He fashioned a most beautiful Garden called Eden that was garnished with all kinds of precious gemstones. It would appear that this garden occupied the entire Earth. This was long before the ocean waters appeared on the Earth. See Figure 1-8. Geological dating methods would indicate that this wonderful and magnificent Archean age lasted in this most beautiful condition for about 800 billion years. See Figure 1-8.

After this time of great jubilation, Lucifer and his angels were brought by God to this beautiful, primordial (First) Garden of Eden from the Third Heaven. It was on Earth that they were able to enjoy and to look after this magnificent Garden. This beautiful garden of Eden is described as follows in Ezekiel 28: 13-14 (NIV), *"13You were in Eden, the garden of God;*

every precious stone adorned you: carnelian, chrysolite and emerald, topaz, onyx and jasper, lapis lazuli, turquoise and beryl. Your settings and mountings were made of gold; on the day you were created they were prepared. ¹⁴You were anointed as a guardian cherub, for so I ordained you. You were on the holy mount of God; you walked among the fiery stones."

The Bible says that Lucifer was able to walk up and down on the stones of fire in the Garden and he was also able to sit in the assembly places of the north before God's Throne on Mount Zion in the Third Heaven. We read in Ezekiel 28:14, *"You were on the Holy Mountain of God."* (NKJV) In other words, Lucifer and his angels were able to commute back and forth from Earth to the Third Heaven just as God's angelic beings are able to do today. They had the best of both worlds.

In this magnificent Primordial Garden of Eden, Lucifer walked on stones of fire. Gemologists tell us that gemstones of great value appear as stones of fire. They have an inert or inner fiery brilliance within them. In other words this Garden was adorned by these beautiful precious gemstones. The grandeur and beauty of this Garden is beyond our very imagination. This was the home of Lucifer and his angels. The Earth at this time would have been a most enticing and wonderful place to visit.

The science of Geology confirms that all the gemstones mentioned above are present within the crystalline rocks of the Archean Age on this Earth. Geology also confirms that there were no oceans present on the Earth during the Archean Age. This would have been during the early part of the First Day of Creation (see Figures 1-1 & 1-8). However, there would have been water in lesser amounts and an atmosphere and hydrosphere suitable for life.

The Fall of Lucifer

One tragic day, sin was found in the heart of Lucifer. The Bible tells us that it was pride that caused Lucifer to rebel against Almighty God. He was a created being of great physical and spiritual beauty. We read in Ezekiel 28:17(NKJV), "*Your heart was lifted up because of your beauty; you corrupted your wisdom for the sake of your splendor.*" Because of his beauty and the splendor of his surroundings, his heart was lifted up in pride. There is an old axiom which says: "*pride comes before the fall*". Sin always begins as a thought, which is later translated into action. Sin always evolves and becomes progressively more evil. This is how it was with Lucifer.

The sin of pride that was conceived in Lucifer's heart began to grow. His sin was soon translated into evil, violent action. Sin corrupted Lucifer's entire being, his body, soul and spirit. He was no longer a creature full of wisdom, but now his wisdom was corrupted and became as foolishness and full of evil. He now realized the great material wealth that he had possessed within this beautiful primordial Garden called Eden. He now wanted to possess it for himself. He commenced a life of sinful pride against Almighty God. Sin always evolves and becomes progressively worse. He, thus, became filled with violence which is recorded as follows: "*By the abundance of your trading, you became filled with violence within and you have sinned.*" (Ezekiel 28:16, NKJV)

Lucifer was no longer the loving, considerate, mild cherub, but now he became as a roaring lion. He was no longer willing to submit his will to the Most High God, but now began to exert his own will and to begin a life of sin in an opposite direction to what he had known before. He wanted everyone to become like himself and he wasn't satisfied until he had caused many of the angels in his realm to likewise commit sin as the following record testifies.

"You have defiled your sanctuaries by the multitude of your iniquities, by the iniquity of your trading." (Ezekie1:28:18, NKJV) The iniquity of trading may indicate that commerce and the exchange of goods of some kind were now also becoming corrupted.

There were sanctuaries in this magnificent Garden of Eden. This is where Lucifer and the hosts of angels under his care and direction used to come to worship Almighty God. It was originally a place of worship, joy, music, and singing. In other words it was a place of paradise, sweet fellowship, reverence and praise to the Most High God. Now his sanctuaries became defiled with the darkness and the blackness of sin. His iniquities became multiplied over and over again as one after another of his angels were deceitfully lured into a life of sin, wickedness, violence and evil against Almighty God.

It is believed that a great number of the angels under Lucifer's jurisdiction were deceived and began living a life of sin and evil. From this moment onward the Earth became a very dark, black, sin-cursed planet.

This tragedy took place at the very end of the Archean Age. It was at this moment in time that God pronounced judgment upon Lucifer and his fallen angels which is described in Ezekiel 28:16-18 (NIV), *"[16]Through your widespread trade you were filled with violence and you sinned. So I drove you in disgrace from the mount of God, and I expelled you, O guardian cherub, from among the fiery stones. [17]Your heart became proud on account of your beauty and you corrupted your wisdom because of your splendor. **So I threw you to the earth**; I made a spectacle of you before kings. [18]By your many sins and dishonest trade you have desecrated your sanctuaries. So I made a fire come out from you, and it consumed you, and **I reduced you to ashes on the ground** in the sight of all who were watching."* Portions of this scripture may refer to past and future judgments of Lucifer by God.

This beautiful primordial Garden of Eden was now removed by God from the Earth. It is believed that God destroyed all evidences of this beautiful Garden by fire and great heat. In other words, the Earth at this moment became a dark, barren, desolate place.

Geologists who have studied the Archean rocks of this age, which I have had the privilege of doing, realize that the Archean Age came to a dramatic termination as a result of great heat. The granitic rocks of this age were in many cases melted and cut by many dark igneous intrusive and volcanic type of rocks and volcanic ash deposits.

It was also at this point in time that Lucifer became known as the Evil One, the Devil and Satan and the fallen angels who followed him became known as demons or evil spirits. God cast them to the Earth into the invisible realm of darkness that now began to surround the Earth. The Bible refers to Satan as a ruler of the air for we read in Ephesians 2:2 that Satan is *"the ruler of the kingdom of the air, the spirit who now is at work in those who are disobedient"* (NIV).

The Demonic Web

Lucifer and his fallen angels were banished to the Demonic Web that now surrounds the Earth. See Figure 1-9. They became the invisible occupants or inhabitants upon the Earth from this time to the present. This Demonic Web belongs to what is called a different "dimension." This is the dimension where the Devil and the hosts of demons dwell and are aware of everything that takes place on the Earth, whereas all animal life and all human life are unable to see them because we are in a different dimension. However, we are all aware of their evil presence and of their evil enticements towards each one of us.

God Judges Lucifer

God pronounced three judgments upon Lucifer just after his fall as follows:

First Judgment: God's first Judgment upon Lucifer is found in Ezekiel 28:16a, NIV "*Through your widespread trade you were filled with violence, and you sinned. So I drove you in disgrace from the Mount of God.*" The reason Lucifer was driven in disgrace from the Mount of God was because he had sinned. Sin is not allowed in God's home which is the Third Heaven. The door to the Third Heaven was shut the instant Lucifer sinned.

Prior to Lucifer's fall, he was able to commute freely from the Earth to the Third Heaven and to sit in the assembly places of the north before the Mount of God. Now Lucifer was no longer free to access the Holy Mount of God in the Third Heaven which is the Mission Control Centre of all Creation. This is where Almighty God is seated on a royal throne high and lifted up on Mount Zion as Isaiah & Ezekiel had the privilege of observing in Isaiah 6:1-3 NIV, and Ezekiel 1:26-28 NIV.

Second Judgment: Lucifer was cast out of the Primordial Garden of Eden, never to return. No longer could he walk up and down in the midst of the beautiful stones of fire. We read, "*I expelled you, O guardian cherub, from among the fiery stones*" (Ezekiel 28:16, NIV). All evidences of this beautiful "Primordial Garden of Eden with all its beautiful gemstones," was at this point in time completely destroyed.

Third Judgment: Lucifer was cast upon the surface of a desolate Earth where the Primordial Garden of Eden had now been removed by fire. We read in Ezekiel 28:17c, NIV "*I threw you to the Earth.*" Then Isaiah 14:12, NIV says, "*How you have fallen from heaven, O morning star, son of the dawn! You have been cast down to the earth.*" The

NKJV says, "*How are you fallen from heaven, O Lucifer, son of the morning! How are you cut down to the ground?*" At this point in time there would have been no oceans as yet. The Earth's surface would have been rocky and desolate as a result of the destruction of the primordial Garden called Eden that possibly encompassed the entire Earth.

The Edenic Curse & the Origin of Death

The Edenic Curse can be traced back to the moment Lucifer sinned. This was the beginning of hardship and death on Earth. From that moment onward, the Earth became a dark sin-cursed planet. We read in Romans 8:20-21(NIV), "*For the creation was subjected to frustration, not by its own choice, but by the will of the one who subjected it, in hope that the creation itself will be liberated from its bondage to decay and brought into the freedom and glory of the children of God.*" As a result of the Edenic Curse every future newly created species of life, after this time, that relate to the bacteria, plant or animal kingdoms on Earth would encounter hardship, suffering, pain, ageing and eventual death. The Earth was no longer a place of perfection, but now because of the Edenic Curse became a place of death and suffering. There would also be violent storms, earthquakes and other natural disasters that would have an adverse affect upon all life on Earth. See Figure 1-1.

Theologians apply the Law of First Reference which says that the first time a word or phrase is found in the book of Genesis or anywhere else in the Bible, that it will give a clue to its meaning later on when its meaning may not be too clear. We find that the first mention of the word "**darkness**" appears in Genesis 1:2 (NKJV), "*And darkness was upon the face of the (roaring) deep.*" In this text, the word darkness is synonymous with evil and the evil one. It implies that the darkness of sin was upon the Earth during the time when the roaring fountains of water began to cover the Earth.

This was when the Birth of the Oceans took place at the commencement of the Proterozoic Age.

The Proterozoic Age Begins

The Proterozoic Age began the moment the Earth became a place of darkness. It was at this point in time that God looked forward through the corridors of time and He foresaw the following events.

First: God foresaw the Birth of the Oceans that would provide the basis for all future events that would take place on Earth.

Second: God foresaw the entire geological history of the Earth from the beginning of the Proterozoic to the present and beyond. He foresaw the millions of species that would one day belong to the bacteria, plant and animal kingdoms. These are the species that he would plan, form and create. These are the plant and animal species that would be able to survive and propagate offspring within a dark, sin cursed Earth. See Figure 1-1.

Thirdly: God foresaw the future Second Garden of Eden and the time when He would one future day form and create Adam & Eve. He would give them the freedom of choice to either follow the Fallen Lucifer or to reject him. He would give the same choice to all their descendents which includes you and I.

Thirdly: God foresaw the Cross. He knew that the only way that He could deal with the sin issue and to eventually eradicate evil on Earth was for his only Son to be one day suspended on a cruel Cross between Heaven and Earth. God the Father ordained that one day in the future, His only begotten Son, the Lord Jesus Christ, would give His body as a sacrifice and would shed His sinless blood for the sins of the world. This was for you and I.

Fourthly: God pronounced the commencement of the Edenic Curse.

The Day & Night Cycle Begins

The Proterozoic Period was the beginning of a new Age. The day and night cycle began at the very beginning of this Age. From this time to the present our Earth has been experiencing day and night, light and darkness. Figures 1-1 and 1-9.

Let us once again read Genesis 1:1-5 NIV, "*In the beginning God created the heavens and the earth. ²Now the earth was formless and empty, **darkness** was over the surface of the deep, and the Spirit of God was hovering over the waters. ³And God said, "Let there be light," and there was light. ⁴God saw that the light was good, and he separated the light from the darkness. ⁵God called the **light** "day," and the **darkness** he called "night."* And there was evening, and there was morning—the first day."

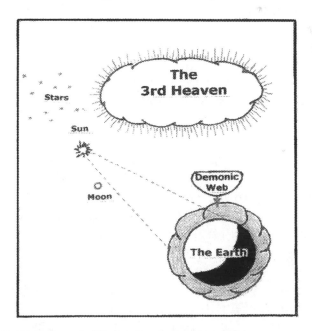

Figure 1-9: The Day & Night Cycle began at the Commencement of the Proterozoic Age. Prepared by Don Daae.

1 John 1:5, says, "*This is the message which we have heard from Him and declare to you, that **God is light and in Him is no darkness at all**.*" If there is no darkness with God, then the darkness that is now described here is the direct result of Lucifer's sin. Lucifer's Fall resulted in the termination of the Archean Age. This was also the beginning of the Proterozoic Age. **Truly, the Fall of Lucifer brought the darkness and the blackness of sin upon the Earth**.

It was at the commencement of the Proterozoic Age that God caused the sun to give light upon the Earth for the first time. God then divided the light from the darkness, giving us day and night. In other words, during the long Archean Age the continuous light upon the Earth came directly from God's throne where there was always continual light. It did not come from the sun. There was no darkness on the Earth prior to the Fall of Lucifer. Figure 1-9.

Geological History of the Proterozoic

The science of geology is a study of the crystalline and the sedimentary rocks on Earth. This study has revealed the continual geological record of water laid sediments from the base of the Proterozoic Period to the present day. See Figure 1-1.

As we continue to open the geological window from the commencement of the Proterozoic Period leading to the time of Early Man, we will begin to realize that the Earth has been very much alive with the multiple appearances of plant and animal life covering a span of about 3+ billion Earth years.

As we progress, we will see that the record of geology and the record of the Bible are astoundingly compatible from the time the Earth was created to the present day.

The Birth of the Oceans

The Proterozoic Age was truly a time of beginning again. The first event that God brought about after the Fall of Lucifer was **the dramatic Birth of the Oceans**. This was in preparation for the eventual appearance of life as we know it today. See Figure 1-10.

The Birth of the Oceans is described in Job 38:7-11 (NIV), *"Who shut up the sea behind doors when it burst forth from the womb, when I made the clouds its garment and wrapped it in **thick darkness**, when I fixed limits for it and set its doors and bars in place, when I said, "This far you may come and no farther; here is where your proud waves halt?"* This sudden appearance of ocean water on the Earth brought the Archean Age to a dramatic close and opened up a new age called the Proterozoic Age. See Figure 1-1.

The Earth's crust is here described as a door capable of holding the waters within the Earth. When the Earth doors were opened, the extremely hot waters from beneath the Earth's crust broke forth as it issued from the womb. The womb implies birth, the birth of the oceans. See Figure 1-10. The Earth's crust went through the excruciating pains as a woman in travail. As a result, the Earth's crust was deformed, mountains and valleys were formed. Continents and ocean areas were established. God made the clouds as a garment and wrapped the Earth in thick darkness. **This darkness was the darkness of sin** that was now present upon the Earth as a result of Lucifer's sin.

The ocean is described as a proud ocean as its waves lapped against the new shore line areas of the Earth. A water cycle and a sophisticated hydrosphere as we know it today was established. The ionosphere was also established to prevent harmful ultraviolet rays from the sun from harming the new chlorophyll generating blue green algae and the bacteria species that were now being created by God in the new water regions of the Earth. The Earth was initially blanketed by a thick cloud bank. In this process God established a greenhouse effect upon the Earth. Truly the Earth was being transformed in preparation for future animal and plant life that could survive upon a sin cursed Earth.

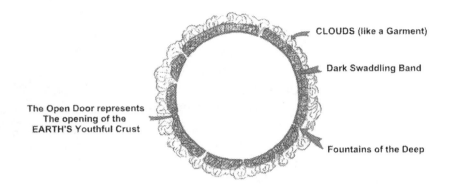

Figure 1-10: The Dramatic Birth of the Oceans. Prepared by Don Daae.

During the birth of the oceans, hydrothermal vents would have been opened through the thin, shifting, crystalline crust, allowing great fountains of molten rock and water to rise to the Earth's surface. The new waters would likely have been in the form of extremely hot water vapor that would have enveloped the Earth as a blanket.

The Earth Sciences of geology and geophysics have revealed amazing information with respect to the dynamics of the Earth's interior. A special edition of Scientific American entitled, "**Our Ever Changing Earth**,"[4] gives a revealing insight into the powerful dynamics within the Earth that are continually changing, shaping and shaking our Earth.

There are those who do not realize the great amount of water that still exists below the Earth's thin crust. A paper presented by Enrico Bonatti[4] in a special edition of Scientific American says, "***The water in earth's mantle could***

equal the amount contained in several oceans." He goes on to say, "*Much of this water is probably primordial, captured in earth's mantle at the time of its formation over four billion years ago.*" In other words there are still great volumes of water remaining within the Earth's interior. This water would be more mobile and readily moveable below the Earth's crust than molten rock called lava.

Geology verifies that the thick cloud bank around the Earth was a short lived event. As the thick layer of clouds dissipated, the Earth experienced a dramatic cooling effect. This precipitated the Earth's first major ice age. Geology calls this ice age the "Gowganda Glaciation." See Figure 1-1.

The Gowganda Glaciation

The Gowganda Glaciation was the first of Five Major Ice Ages that have been identified on Earth. I personally believe that the primary purpose of this Glacial Ice Age and later ice ages was for the purpose of rejuvenating and cleansing the environment in preparation for the creation of new plant and animal life on Earth that was to follow.

David Lindsey[5] describes the evidences of this Ice Age as follows, "*The Gowganda Formation is part of the thick Huronián sequence of Precambrian sedimentary rocks that crop out in central Ontario from Lake Superior to Quebec. Although it has long been considered to be glacial, recent work on submarine slump and turbidite deposits has reopened the question of its origin. This study was made to determine its origin and paleogeography.*" Then he says, "*Till-like conglomerates, varved argillites, and abundant dropstones characterize the Gowganda and provide strong evidence for a glacial origin. Pebble fabric parallel to regional paleocurrents, rare striated and grooved pavements, and abundant unweathered detritus are also in harmony with a glacial origin. Local thin-bedded sandstones contain flame structure, graded bedding, contorted bedding, and rippled tops, suggesting deposition by turbidity flows. Association of these sandstones with varved argillites and rafted stones indicates that Gowganda turbidites are glaciolacustrine.*" I would advise the reader to go to Google to get additional information.

It is reported that the rocks called Gowganda conglomerates include striated boulders as large as 10 feet (3.048 m) across. These are also overlain by tillites locally up to 600 feet (182.9 m) in thickness. All of these glacial sediments are of very early Proterozoic Age. They lie directly upon crystalline rocks of the Archean Age.

Proterozoic Sediments

The Proterozoic sediments are Earth's oldest water laid sediments. It is obvious even at this early point in time that the ocean basin regions were already separated from the highland continental regions. The ocean waters naturally filled the lower topographic regions.

The continental regions consisted of the granite crystalline Archean type of rocks plus the newly intruded darker igneous basalts, andesites and other volcanic lavas and ash deposits. These rocks came under intense erosion by water. This resulted in the deposition of Earth's first sediments in the newly formed offshore regions.

The Proterozoic age spans about 3.3 billion Earth years. It was during this long period of time that God began creating within the waters, the first species in the form of bacteria and chlorophyll generating algae. He was also in the process of establishing a sophisticated food chain in preparation for the creation of future animal life.

For example, in the vicinity of Lake Louise, Alberta and Field, BC in the Rocky Mountains west of Calgary, Alberta in Canada, the total water laid sediments of Proterozoic age increase in thickness westward to about 20,000 feet (6,096m) thick in the Field, B.C. region. This unit increases to over 30,000 feet+ (9,144 meters+) in thickness to the west of Golden, British Columbia. See Figure 1-10. The immense thicknesses of these sediments reveal the great amount of time that was involved in their deposition.

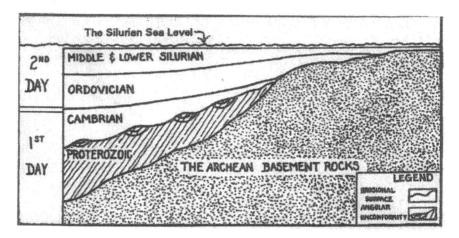

Figure 1-11: Is a schematic cross section of the Proterozoic and Cambrian sediments west of Calgary, Alberta Canada. They are overlying the crystalline basement rocks of Archean Age. Please relate to Figure 1-1. Figure by Don Daae.

The overlying Cambrian sediments increase in thickness in a westward direction from Calgary, Alberta to about 10,000 feet (3,048m) in the vicinity of Field, BC. These sediments continue to increase in thickness in a westward direction from Field, BC. See Figures 1-11 & 1-12.

The First Appearance of Plant Life & Bacteria

Plant and animal life require water and bacteria in order to survive. Geology confirms the presence of ocean water at the very beginning of the Proterozoic Age. Geology also confirms that these oldest Proterozoic sediments contain life in the form of bacteria and blue green algae. Where did the bacteria and algae come from? Did they evolve by an unintelligent, evolutionary process or were they created and formed by an Almighty Creator God? Figure 1-1.

Blue green algae are prokaryote chlorophyll generating water plants. They first appear at the base of the Proterozoic sediments together with species of bacteria. The more complex eukaryotic green algae appear during the mid portion of this age. Then the eukaryotic red and brown algae appear near the upper portions of the Proterozoic.

Once the different algae species appear, they have continued to propagate themselves practically unchanged to the present. The fact that they appear suddenly in the fossil record, fully developed and specialized, gives credence to Special Creation. **Barghoorn**[6] stated, "*Many living species [algae & bacteria] are almost indistinguishable in structure from species that flourished a billion or more years ago.*" Towards the end of the Proterozoic Age, the oceans of the Earth were essentially modern. God was in the process of establishing a luxuriant food chain in preparation for the soon arrival of the first animal life. The big event that preceded the first animal life was a pronounced cooling of the climate and the commencement of a second major Ice Age.

Late Proterozoic Ice Age

The largest and most extensive Glaciation (Ice Age) that the Earth has ever experienced took place during the Upper Proterozoic Age. See Figures 1-11 and 1-12. Evidences of this major Glaciation have been found throughout the globe, including the British Isles, Scandinavia, Greenland, The United States, Africa, northeast Asia, South America and Australia, This Ice Age ranks as one of the outstanding and exceptional events in the history of the Earth.

Max D. Crittenden Jr. and Nocholas Christi Buck and Paul Karl Link[7] did extensive work on temperature variations within sediments of Proterozoic Age. This work was done in the western regions of the USA to the south of Alberta, Canada. They say, *"A record of glaciation during late Proterozoic time is preserved in a number of localities extending from the Sheeprock Mountains, Utah, to Pocatello, Idaho, and from the Park City area 25 miles (40 km) east of Salt Lake City to the Deep Creek Range along the Utah-Nevada line. Over much of this area, the glacial deposits and associated rocks thicken westward and form the basal part of a miogeoclinal wedge that accumulated near the late Proterozoic and early Paleozoic continental margin."*[7]

What they are describing is analogous to how these same Proterozoic sediments thicken westward from Calgary, Alberta. See Figure 1-11. They go on to say, *"There is evidence for two pulses of Glaciation during the Late Proterozoic in northern Utah and southwestern Idaho."*[7]

If two separate episodes of Glaciation are evident to the south of Canada in the USA, then our Canadian glacial geologists should be critically examining our Proterozoic sediments in the Rocky Mountains and the Interior Mountains to the west of Golden, B.C. to find these two glacial events in Canada.

They go on to say, *"In the east, such deposits are thin and rest on Archean basement or rocks of Proterozoic age; in the west, they are part of thicker sequences in which deposition apparently continued without significant interruption from late Proterozoic into Cambrian time. In many places, the original continuity between the western and eastern parts of the depositional wedge has been obscured by thrusting of Cretaceous and early Tertiary age that carried the thick basinal sequences eastward over those deposited on the continental platform."*[7]

As stated earlier. I personally believe that the main purpose for these two major Proterozoic Glaciations (Ice Ages) were to have a rejuvenating and cleansing effect upon the Earth's environment. This was in preparation for the creation of new life that followed each of these two major Ice Ages. See Figures 1-1, 1-12.

The First Animal Life

Within the upper portion of the Proterozoic sediments, scientists have found the first evidence of animal life. A distinct species of a **jelly fish, a sponge, traces of worm burrowing and traces of shelly fragments** that possibly relate to a fourth phyla have been found. These 4 species represent the first appearance of 4 new animal phyla on planet Earth. They appeared just after the termination of the Upper Proterozoic Ice Age. See Figure 1-12.

Geology has confirmed that life in the form of bacteria and algae are present throughout the Proterozoic sediments from bottom to top. Evidences of life have been destroyed where the sediments have undergone later metamorphic processes resulting from great heat and pressure generated by mountain building processes and hot intrusive lava and magmas that have cut through the sediments. However, where these sediments have not undergone these destructive diagenetic changes, then bacteria and algae are found throughout the long Proterozoic Age.

The Cambrian Age

The Cambrian geological window is shown on Figure 1-12. The Cambrian Period began about 544 million years ago and ended about 510 million years ago, an interval of about 34 million years. The extraordinary event called the Cambrian Explosion of Animal Life took place during the Lower Cambrian Period about midway between 525 and 530 million years ago as shown on Figure 1-12. This represents a short period of 5 million years. Geologists refer to the Cambrian Explosion of Animal life as having taken place within a geological instant. Chlorophyll generating plant life in the form of algae supplied food for the new species of animal life.

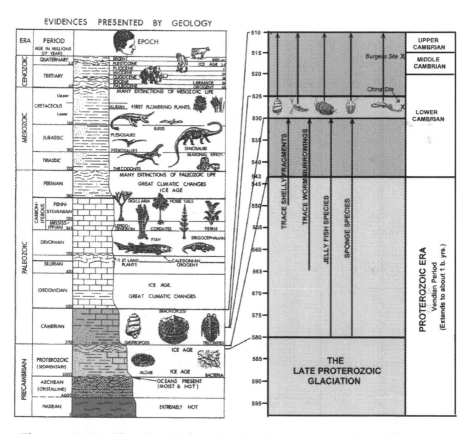

Figure 1-12: The Cambrian Explosion of Animal Life Window is shown within sediments of Lower Cambrian Age from 525-530 million years ago. The first four animal species on Earth appeared prior to this time and after the most grandiose Ice Age the Earth has ever experienced. Compare with Figures 1-1 & 1-4. Figure by Don Daae and computer generated by Mike Gilders.

The Cambrian Explosion of Animal Life

The Cambrian Explosion of Animal Life refers to the moment in time when a sudden burst of new animal life made their first appearance on the Earth. The December, 1995 issue of Time magazine entitled this event, "When Life Exploded." It described the sudden explosion of animal life as an amazing frenzy that changed our Earth overnight.

The Cambrian Explosion of Animal Life is indeed one of the most significant events that took place in the animal world. It has also caused scientists throughout the world to re-examine their traditionally held interpretations of life on Earth.

Many leading scientists are saying that anywhere from 40+ disparate (completely different) architectural animal body plans (phyla) came into existence during the Lower Cambrian. The late paleontologist and expert on Cambrian animal life Stephen J. Gould[8] says, *"Some fifteen to twenty Burgess species cannot be allied with any known group, and should probably be classified as separate phyla."* Gould and other leading scientists are saying that it is reasonable to say that 46+ phyla were present at the time of the Cambrian Explosion of Animal life.

A leading British paleontologist Simon Conway Morris[9] has done exhaustive studies on the Burgess Fauna. He says, *"The concept of the phylum is generally taken to be basic to our understanding of animals inasmuch as each of the phyla corresponds to one of the 35 or so basic body plans identified today."*

At the end of the Cambrian Period there was a major worldwide extinction of animal phyla. From that time forward only 35 or so animal phyla have continued to the present. There is disagreement among some scientists as to what constitutes a phyla or sub-phyla and as to the number of phylum that came into being at the time of the Cambrian Explosion. This will take time to sort out.

BACTERIA KINGDOM	PLANT KINGDOM	ANIMAL KINGDOM
PHYLA (BODY PLANS)	PHYLA BODY PLANS	PHYLA BODY PLANS
	Class	Class
	Order	Order
	Family	Family
	Genus	Genus
SPECIES	SPECIES	SPECIES

Figure 1-13: A Simple Taxonomy Chart. God only created species. He related each species to a certain body plan or Phyla.

In order to understand the sudden appearance of animal life, it is necessary to define what is a phylum? What is a species? What do we mean by Taxonomy? What is a body Plan?

What Is Taxonomy?

Taxonomy is an artificial system created by man to place all species into groupings such as genus, family, group, order, class for purposes of filing, storing and categorizing all life. All animal life, macro and micro, can be categorized into one of three known Kingdoms.

There is the Animal Kingdom, the Plant Kingdom and the Third Kingdom in which are found bacteria and viruses. Now no species of animal or plant life could survive apart from the life given to them from the Third Kingdom, which we will call, for the sake of simplification, the **Bacteria/Virus Kingdom**. The life within each kingdom is known by multi individual species that relate to that kingdom. The above Taxonomy Chart shows the species category to be located at the bottom of a certain Kingdom, whereas the phyla are at the top. See Figure 1-13.

What is a Species?

When analyzing the life within the three Kingdoms, only a species by definition has the ability to reproduce fertile offspring from generation to generation. In other words, all animal life on Earth today, together with all animal life that has ever lived, belong to a specific species. Every species has a unique body plan called a phylum. Each animal species come under the umbrella of one of the 40 to 45+ phyla that scientists have identified from the Cambrian Explosion of Animal Life. Today there are only about 35 or so phyla that have managed to survive the first known extinction of animal life at the end of Cambrian Period.

The artificial groupings such as genus, family, order, class, etc., between a species and a phylum were already in place at the time when each animal species came into existence. Taxonomy did not evolve as evolutionists would make us believe. Throughout geological time God only created new species and each species was created according to a preconceived plan. Each new species was created to fit into one of the body plans (phyla) that was established when animal life first began. The wonder of it all is that each species is unique and different from every other of the multi thousands of species that have been identified within the geological column. Could an undirected, unintelligent evolutionary process achieve such a remarkable task? Definitely not. Could a highly intelligent, all knowing, ever present Creator God achieve this remarkable task? The answer is an overwhelming yes. Every paleontologist, palynologists and geologist depends upon the fossil record in order to determine the specific geological age of the Earth. See Figure 1-1.

What is a Phylum?

A Phylum constitutes the highest biological category in the Animal, Plant or Bacteria Kingdoms. Each individual phylum exhibits a unique architectural blue print or novel structural design that is called a body plan. For instance, Man belongs to the Chordate Phylum. The Chordate Phylum is characterized by an animal that has a vertebral column with a notochord. **This constitutes a unique body plan.** All vertebrate animals with a vertebral column and a notochord such as birds, fish, amphibians, reptiles and mammals belong to the Chordate Phylum.

The Chordate Body Plan is one of 35 or so distinct animal body plans, micro and macro, that scientists have identified as being present in our modern world. However, there were 40+, some scientists say 47+ phyla, or distinct body plans present during the Cambrian Period. The species that belonged to these extra phyla mysteriously disappeared at the end of the Cambrian Age.

How Can a Phylum Relate to Man?

In order to simply explain how a Phylum can relate to Man, I often use this well known simple analogy. In my lecture classes, I emphasize that every person in my class has a back bone. This means that each person has a vertebral column with a notochord. Therefore it represents the body plan that in this case relates to the Chordate Phylum. During the Cambrian Explosion of Animal life, there was a little animal that God created that had a vertebral column with a notochord. This chordate body plan is called a Phylum by scientists. See Figure 1-13. This also means that every animal that God created from the Cambrian Explosion of Animal Life to the present that has a vertebral column with a spinal cord belongs in the Chordate Phylum. This means that all fish, amphibians, reptiles and mammals are all members of the Chordate Phylum or Body Plan. This has nothing to do with evolution, but has everything to do with God's creative plan for the chordate phylum.

How a Body Plan Relates to Inventions of Man

Many scientists have compared an animal body plan to a certain invention of Man in order to clarify what a body plan really means. For instance, all boats have a unique and novel body plan. The first boat that was ever constructed by Early Man probably involved the scooping out of the inner part of a large tree trunk to form a boat. Now, this boat consisted of a hull and a simple paddle to propel the boat in the water. All future boats have a similar body plan. They all have a hull and a method of propelling their boat from place to place. This would apply to large ocean liners, passenger ships, small and large boats of every sort and kind. Another illustration often given is that of an automobile. The first automobile had four wheels and a chassis plus an engine for propulsion. Every automobile since that time has a similar body plan. Airplanes also have a novel and unique body plan. The first airplane built by the Wright Brothers had a body, tail, two wings and an engine for propulsion. Every airplane model since that time has the same four component parts. Yet each airplane model is unique and different.

Man was the designer and creator of each succeeding model of a boat, car or airplane. Every new model is distinctly different from the previous model. This has nothing to do with one boat evolving into another boat or one car evolving into another car or one airplane evolving into another airplane. It is all about the intelligence and genius of the inventor who designed and created each new model after the original body plan and with unique features that would satisfy a certain human need.

When God created the first clam it had a unique body plan that related to the Mollusk Phylum. It was designed by the Great Intelligent Designer or Architect of the Universe, God the Father, to satisfy a certain ecological need on Earth. It was created by God the Son according to the architectural blueprint. It was maintained and nourished by the Great Divine Indweller of the Universe who is God the Holy Spirit. See Figure 1-3. The succeeding thousands of clam species found within the fossil record are each unique and different, yet they all belong to the original Mollusk Phylum.

Likewise when God designed, created and formed Man, He placed Man into the Chordate Phylum. Adam & Eve were designed by the Master Architect of the Universe. They were formed and created by the Master Creator according to the Master Plan. It is interesting to note that there is only one species of Man on this Earth called Homo sapiens. Every human being regardless of the color of their skin or race belongs to the same species. They all have a vertebral column with a notochord. The wonder of it all is that every human being is unique and different from every other human being. This reveals the great diversity within a species.

Animal Life Before the Cambrian Explosion

Three definite animal species representing three separate phyla have been identified prior to the Cambrian Explosion. They are a sponge, a jellyfish and a certain worm species. A fossil species identified by trace, shelly fragments, represents a possible fourth phylum. See Figure 1-13.

A sponge species has been identified in late Proterozoic sediments. This sponge is well documented at the Weng'an site in southern China. The Upper Proterozoic sediments at this site are remarkably well preserved with very little or no metamorphic damage. Phosphate is present which gives these sediments very good preservation potential. Evidence of seaweeds (algae) are abundant and very well preserved. Heeren[11] relates how paleontologist Jun-Yuan Chen and Taiwanese cell biologist Chia-Wei Li discovered sponges in a 580 million year old layer. This was the oldest discovery of multicellular animals in the world.

This sponge can be traced back in the fossil record to about 580 million years ago to the latter part of the Upper Proterozoic Age. See Figure 1-12.

Jelly Fish species: Heeren[10] relates how Caltech biologist Eric Davidson has now identified cnidarian-like embryos among Chen's Weng'an specimens in China, indicating that jellyfish-like animals were living in the Upper Proterozoic about 580 million years ago. See Figure 1-12. It looked very much like a modern Jelly Fish.

A Worm species: Upper Proterozoic trails, called **trace fossils**, indicate the presence of some kind of simple worm slithering through the mud during the Upper Proterozoic Age. No actual worms have been found. See Figure 1-12.

Small shelly fauna: Traces of small shelly fauna have been found in Late Proterozoic and Lower Cambrian sediments from about 550 to 530 million years ago. See Figure 1-12. It is believed that this animal species would represent a fourth phyla. Gould[11] says, "*the first fauna of hard parts, called the Tommotian after a locality in Russia (but also world-wide in extent), contains some creatures with identifiably modern design, but most of its members are tiny blades, caps, and cups of uncertain affinity—the small shelly fauna, we paleontologists call it, with honorable frankness and definite embarrassment.*"[11]

All of the above four species appeared after a major **Global Ice Age** that is recorded in the latter part of the Proterozoic Period. This Ice Age ended about 680 million years ago. It is believed to have acted as a cleansing and rejuvenating influence upon the environment in preparation for the first animal life.

Ediacarean Fossils: Between 680 to 543 million years ago just after this major Proterozoic global Ice Age, geologists discovered the first appearance of Ediacarian Fossils (Figure 1-11). They were named after the town of Ediacara in South Australia. Imprints of strange soft-bodied organisms were found in sandstone beds. **Up to now, they have been mistakenly identified as animal remains.** These fossils have been traditionally viewed as some type of sea-pens and or marine worms. They are commonly disk or feather shaped. They became extinct at the end of the Proterozoic Age. They are unrelated to any modern animals.

Ediacarean fossils have been identified in Canada and at various other parts of the world. Heeren[12] says, *"Before the sponge discoveries, some still believed that the strange frond, disks, and blades provided the best hope for finding the Cambrian's animal ancestors. This was the closest thing to faunal variety found in the Precambrian Era. **In his symposium talk, German Ediacarean specialist Michael Steiner concluded that the flat, air-mattress-like Ediacareans looked more like well-organized colonies of lichen than any kind of Cambrian animal.**"* Chinese paleontologists are now classifying the Ediacarean fossils as a type of algae.

Animal Life After the Cambrian Explosion

At *"The Origin of Animal Body Plans and the Fossil Record* International Symposium" at Chengjiang, China in June/July 1999, it was noted that there were no "new" body plans (phyla) after the Cambrian Period. There are about 35 or so animal phyla present on Earth today. During Cambrian time, there were 40+ body plans. Each phylum was represented by one or more individual species. Some scientists claim there may have been as many as 47+ phyla (unique body plans). It becomes obvious that at the end of Cambrian time, many of these phyla became extinct. This is the first geological record of a major extinction of animal life on planet Earth.

Where are the Cambrian Fossils Found?

They are found in Cambrian sediments at many places throughout the Earth. However, there are two places in the world, the Chengjiang Site in southern China and the Burgess Shale Site at Field, BC in Western Canada, where these fossils have been remarkably preserved.

The Chengjiang Fossil Site in China

The Chengjiang Fossil Site is located in the southern province of Yunnan in China. This site contains the oldest and best preserved Cambrian fossils in the world. The geological setting is much different from Field, B.C. in Canada. In China, the sedimentary layers are mostly horizontal. They have not experienced severe tectonic or great earth movements during periods of mountain building. Paul Chien PhD[13] personally relayed to me that Professor J.W. Chen, a very knowledgeable scientist from China, believed the Lower Cambrian marine animals were living in a shallow water environment. During storm conditions they were swept into deeper water along a submarine slope. Layers of yellow silt and clay buried the animals quickly. The animals were thus hidden from scavengers and protected from decomposing bacteria and predators. The fossils were not deformed as a result of differential compaction of thick overlying sediments or from the stress resulting from dramatic mountain building. The Cambrian sediments went through low temperature diagenetic processes, thus the fossils are remarkably well preserved.

This special site has thick continuous sequences of underlying Cambrian and Proterozoic sediments. Chinese geologists, palynologists, paleontologists are able to identify the exact time during the Lower Cambrian age when the "Cambrian

Explosion of Animal Life" took place. This is in contrast to Field, B.C. where the Cambrian fossils are preserved only in the Middle Cambrian Stephen Shale Formation. Many of the same species and phyla are found at both sites. This indicates that these animals were cosmopolitan and present worldwide. See Figure 1-12.

The Burgess Shale Fossil Site in Canada

The famous Burgess Shale fossil site in Canada is located on Mt Stephen on the north side of the town of Field, B.C. in the beautiful Canadian Rocky Mountains of Western Canada. The famous Walcott Quarry of Cambrian fossils was first discovered by Charles Doolittle Walcott in 1907. This quarry and several nearby quarries to the north and south of the town of Field B.C., have yielded a wealth of Middle Cambrian fossils that relate to the so-called, "Cambrian Explosion of Animal Life."

These fossils are found in a bed of dark gray to black shale called "The thick Stephen Shale Formation." Figure 1-14 illustrates the geology at Field, B.C.

Dr. Charles Walcott discovered the most prolific fossil quarry site along the Fossil Ridge during his intense field work between the years 1907 to 1924. It is called the Walcott Quarry of Cambrian Age. Both hard and soft body fossils were found. The best soft body fossils are found in a 2.3 meter (7.4 foot) thick bed called the "Phyllopod Bed." These fossils are remarkably preserved. Since then, additional fossil beds have been discovered above and below the Walcott quarry. Burgess Shale is a term that Walcott applied to all fossils that directly relate to these mysterious Cambrian fossils.

Geology at Field, B.C.

During the Cambrian Period of time, this region of Western Canada was at the western edge of an ancient Middle and

Upper Cambrian shoreline that angled in a northwest / southeast direction. The sediments to the NE of this shoreline were shallow water carbonates, whereas the sediments to the SW were deep water basin shale type of sediments that are illustrated on Figure 1-14.

The geology at Field, B.C. consists primarily of sedimentary rock layers of Lower, Middle and Upper Cambrian age. The Lower Cambrian strata at this location is underlain by about 6,100 meters (20,000 feet) of older Proterozoic sediments that thicken westward into British Columbia to 9100+ meters (30,000+ feet) in places. These older marine, water laid sediments have experienced various degrees of metamorphism, which have destroyed all evidences of Proterozoic life. See Figure 1-1.

Cambrian Sediments at Field, B.C.

The total Cambrian sediments overlying the Proterozoic sediments are in the vicinity of 3,000 meters (10,000 feet) in thickness at Field, BC. They continue to thicken in a southwesterly direction. Let us now examine these Cambrian age sediments at Field, B.C.

The Gog Group of Lower Cambrian Age

During the Lower Cambrian Age vast deposits of "beach sands" of about 2,000 meters (6560 feet) thick known as the Gog Group were deposited above the eroded surface of underlying Proterozoic sediments. See Figures 1-1 & 1-14.

It is interesting to observe that in the eastern Rocky Mountain region of Canada, there is almost always an erosion surface that separates the older Proterozoic sediments from the above Cambrian age sediments. This is an interesting mystery. It is obvious that the Creator brought the Proterozoic Age to a dramatic close prior to initiating the overlying sediments of the Gog Group that are of Lower Cambrian Age.

By early Middle Cambrian time the Cathedral Formation carbonates were deposited. They consist of shallow water algal carbonates. These carbonates form an impressive carbonate bank edge that was in filled to the west by offshore deeper water dark gray silts and shale's of the Lower Chandler Group of Formations. This Carbonate Bank edge represents a hinge line that separated the thicker basinal marine clay sediments to the southwest from the more shallow water "Platform Carbonates" to the northeast. Figure 1-14 reveals that this hinge line was oriented in a northwest/southeast direction as Cambrian time progressed.

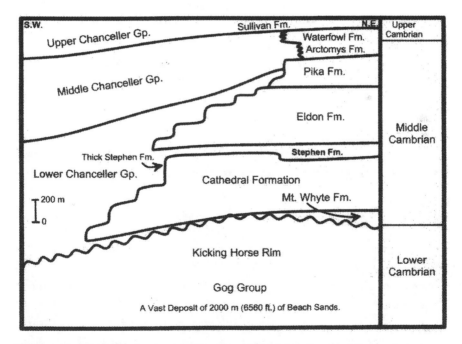

Figure 1-14: Illustrates how the Stephen Formation relates to the entire Cambrian stratigraphic section at Field, B.C. "The Burgess Shale Fossils" are only found in the so called "Thick Stephen Formation." This figure was patterned after that of Murray Coppold and Wayne Powell who are the authors of "A

Geoscience Guide to the Burgess Shale." [14] **This figure was prepared by Don Daae & computer drawn by Mike Gilders.**

The Burgess Shale Fossils

The very important Stephen Formation contains the famous Burgess Shale fossils at Field, BC. It is a marine fairly thin shallow water dark grey shale unit that lies above the Cathedral Carbonates. The Stephen Shale unit also extends westward over the Cathedral escarpment. Coppold and Powell[15] say, "*A recent re-interpretation suggests that the escarpment is the headwall of a regional slide scar, where the over-steepened front of the Cathedral Formation carbonates are older than the adjacent mudstones of the Stephen Formation.*" See Figure 1-14.

Coppold and Powell[16] say, "*The Stephen Formation is much thinner on top of the escarpment than below it. With little creativity, geologists refer to these rocks as 'thin Stephen Formation' and 'thick Stephen Formation' respectively. The Cathedral Escarpment marks this change and can be traced across much of Yoho National Park.*" Fossils are only found in the thick Stephen Formation. These fossils are now referred to as the **"Burgess Shale Fossils."**

Geology reveals that this vertical carbonate submarine cliff is over 100 meters (328 feet) high. At this ancient time, it is believed that Cambrian marine animals were living in the shallow waters above the Cathedral Carbonates. During storm conditions these animals were swept seaward over this escarpment into 100+ meters (330+ feet) of water where they were simultaneously covered with muddy clays. The animals were thus hidden from scavengers. They were oxygen starved, and protected from decomposing bacteria and predators. This cliff also protected these animals from destruction by later differential compaction due to the weight of overlying sediments that geologists have estimated to have been in the order of 10,000+ meters (32,000+ feet) of younger age sediments that later experienced deposition, subsequent erosion and mountain building.

Coppold and Powell[17] say, *"This submarine cliff was crucial to fossil formation and preservation in the Burgess Shale: no Cathedral Escarpment, no fossils."* They go on to say, *"But there is a lot more to it than a simple lack of oxygen, as many bacteria can decompose an animal without it. In fact, almost every animal keeps a supply within its gut; every carcass comes complete with everything necessary to break it down."* They then say *"Some paleontologists believe that the answer to the preservation puzzle lies in the rock surrounding the fossils. The mudstones consist almost entirely of clay."* Coppold and Powell[18] say, *"As a result of turbulent deposition, the fossils were not laid down flat. Instead many lie at odd angles to the sedimentary layers, with clay separating each delicate appendage and forced into every crack and crevice (including the gut). The clay intercalations inhibited decomposition, leaving the thin films that define the Burgess Shale fossils today."* They then say[19], *"Proximity to the buttressing escarpment is what may have saved the Burgess fossils from destruction in subsequent rock-sharing episodes of compaction under ten kilometers of younger sediment and subsequent exhumation and mountain building."*

The late naturalist Stephen J. Gould[20] summed it up by saying, *"The preservation of the Burgess Shale fossils is a miracle."* It is indeed a miracle of God that these fossils are so well preserved. In some cases, even soft body parts such as the digestive tract, muscle fiber, and gut are still preserved.

Interpretation of the Burgess Shale Fossils

At present there are four major interpretation categories to explain the Cambrian Explosion of animal life. They are:

1. Neo-Darwinian Interpretation.
2. Punctuated Equilibrium Interpretation.
3. An Intelligent Design Interpretation.
4. A Bible-Based Interpretation.

There are two primary secular interpretations that attempt to explain the origin of animal species that relate to the Cambrian Explosion. They are the Neo-Darwinian Interpretation and the Punctuated Equilibrium Interpretation. They both deny the existence of an all powerful, intelligent, creative God.

Neo-Darwinian Interpretation

This Interpretation is based upon the premise that each species has gradually evolved from a previous species by an unintelligent, undirected, chance evolutionary process over a long period of time. It refers to a particular naturalistic mechanism that produces descent with modification through successive generations. This mechanism maintains that new species are formed by natural selection acting upon random (genetic) variations or mutations. It implies that new species arise as a result of a steady transformation of its ancestors.

To date, this mechanism can only explain variations within the genetic boundary of a species. Scientists refer to this variation as **microevolution**. For example, it can explain variations of beak size among the finches of the Galapagos Islands, but each variation is still a finch. However, it cannot explain the vast difference between a finch and a robin; that is, between one species and another species.

Macroevolution is the neo-Darwinian term to explain how one species has evolved into another species. Many scientists are now seriously questioning whether the Darwinian Mechanism can produce macroevolution or the amount of change required to account for the development of new species or of the great numbers of uniquely different body plans (phyla) that suddenly emerged within a geologic instant about 530 million years ago (Figures 1-1, 1-5, & 1-12).

Neo-Darwinists have failed to explain the origin of uniquely different body plans called phyla and the sudden appearance of associated species during the Lower Cambrian Explosion of animal life. They have failed to explain the sudden appearance of each new species of animal life throughout the geological history of the Earth. They have also failed to explain how male and female species could have evolved by chance simultaneously and separately to ensure the propagation of each species.

Is this the reason why the Cambrian Explosion of Animal life is being kept a secret from the public? Today, the public knows very little or practically nothing about this most important biological dramatic event. Is this a deliberate concealment of scientific evidences?

Are Species Complex?

The first recorded species found in the lowermost Proterozoic Age sediments are blue green algae and bacteria. Where did they come from? Yes, they are complex. Did the bacteria evolve from the blue green algae? Or is it more reasonable to believe that the multi species of bacteria and algae were created by an all powerful Creator God according to a pre-conceived ecological plan.

Evolutionary scientists often refer to bacteria as simple and primitive forms of life. However, scientists today are realizing the intricate complexities of bacteria. Dr. Michael Behe[21] describes a certain bacteria species as having three component parts, a paddle, a rotor and a motor. It is like a sophisticated motor where the moving parts can move the bacteria at great speed. He was able to verify that if one particular component fails, the entire bacteria becomes dysfunctional causing the bacteria to die. It was, therefore, impossible for a bacteria species to have evolved by the addition of new component parts as Darwinists maintain.

The reconstruction of a bacteria flagellum by Behe illustrates the complexity of what Darwinists refer to as the most simple, primitive form of life. Behe reveals that a bacteria flagellum is not simple.

Theory of Irreducible Complexity

Michael J. Behe[22] expanded upon the Theory of Irreducible Complexity. "*It states that an irreducible biological system, such as a bacteria species, is made up of well matched interdependent parts. In order for it to function all parts had to have been fully formed and synchronized in place. It was impossible for the separate parts to have evolved in isolation from each other accumulating their characteristics one by one over a period of time to make a healthy organism.*"

In his book, "Darwin's Black Box," Michael Behe describes the utter futility of gradual evolution ever taking place in the bacteria, animal or plant kingdoms. He emphasizes the fact that **all living organisms are irreducibly complex.** The question arises what do scientists believe as being irreducibly complex? Behe then describes what is meant by a biological system that is irreducibly complex. Behe[23] says, "*By irreducibly complex I mean a single system composed of several well matched, interacting parts that contribute to the basic function, wherein the removal of any one of the parts causes the system to effectively cease functioning. An irreducibly complex system cannot be produced directly (that is, by continuously improving the initial function, which continues to work by the same mechanism) by slight, successive modifications of a precursor system, because any precursor to an irreducibly complex system that is missing a part is by definition nonfunctional. An irreducibly complex biological system, if there is such a thing, would be a powerful challenge to Darwinian evolution.*"

The Theory of Irreducible Complexity can be applied to all species that belong to the Bacteria, Animal and the Plant Kingdoms. It is now possible to demonstrate that every species is made up of well matched major interdependent parts. This ensures that it was impossible for the separate major parts to have evolved in isolation from each other accumulating their characteristics one by one over a period of time to make a healthy organism.

This does not mean that a bacteria species will not eventually die. Every bacteria species is born for a specific plan and purpose. It will reproduce new bacteria. Once this plan is accomplished, it will die.

The same is true of every species of animal, plant, bacteria or virus forms of life. Every species that has ever existed in the past has lived and died. Paleontologists, biologists and palynologists have analyzed and described the many thousands of species. There is a mystery surrounding the death of all life. What is the origin of death, pain, suffering and hardship that all animal, plant and bacteria species encounter during their brief time on Earth? In simple terms, the origin of death, pain and suffering is the result of Lucifer's Fall at the end of the Archean Age. **His fall resulted in the Edenic Curse** that has affected all aspects of life on Earth up to the present day. We can be thankful that this curse will come to an end at a certain future day.

Does the Fossil Record Support Neo-Darwinism?

The fossil record does **not** support the Neo-Darwinian interpretation. Since Darwin's day, multi billions of dollars have been spent by oil companies, mining companies, government agencies and research centers to geologically explore the Earth's resources onshore and offshore. A vast amount of geological knowledge has been obtained.

Geologists, palynologists, paleontologists, biologists and supporting scientists have carefully analyzed the fossil assemblages within the geological column worldwide. Geological field parties have taken detailed samples of geological formations throughout the world. Drilling samples and cored intervals of countless wells have been carefully analyzed. Scientists from countries around the world have met to share their information. The geological and other scientific findings strongly confirm that each species appears suddenly in the fossil record fully formed. The transitional forms that are essential to neo-Darwinism are not to be found.

Darwin maintained that if it could be demonstrated that any complex organ existed that could not possibly have been formed by numerous, successive, slight modifications then, his theory would absolutely break down. The evidence of science, through the Theory of Irreducible Complexity, verifies that Darwin's Theory has absolutely broken down.

In spite of this geological and biological fact, ardent Neo-Darwinists continue to falsely insist that evolution is a fact of science. They continue to blindly live in a world of denial. They continue to falsely indoctrinate students at our universities, colleges and schools to believe in a pseudo evolutionary science that is not based on factual scientific evidence, but is based upon the religious teachings of Naturalism, Secular Humanism and Atheism.

During my career, I have worked closely with many major and independent oil and gas companies. I have had the privilege of working closely with specialists in paleontology, palynology and geology. I have also attended many management meetings discussing the findings and deciding where a well should be drilled. In all these years, I have yet to hear a President or any top Manager of Exploration ever ask the following question when deciding where a well should be drilled: what does evolution have to say?

In fact, in the practical world, evolution has nothing that is scientifically sound to say. It is only in the institutions of higher learning that Darwinists insist that evolution has something to say. This is where our students are being continually brainwashed into thinking that evolution is a fact of science.

The Neo-Darwinian Mystery

A mystery surrounds the neo-Darwinian Interpretation. They fail to explain where the 40+ phyla (body plans) identified with the Cambrian Explosion have come from. If the neo-Darwinian Interpretation is true, then it demands the presence of hard and soft-bodied ancestral animal fossil remains throughout the great thicknesses of underlying Cambrian and Proterozoic water laid sediments. See Figures 1-14 and 1-1.

The argument is presented by Darwinists that the ancestors of all Cambrian Explosion body plans (phyla) may have had soft body parts, thus were never preserved. It is interesting to note that the great numbers of bacteria and algae (sea weed & plankton), sponges and jelly fish species were largely soft bodied and are preserved in the fossil record within the thick underlying Cambrian and Proterozoic sediments in China and in all other parts of the world. This makes it hard to believe that the Cambrian Explosion fossils, some of which are soft bodied organisms should not have been preserved in conjunction with the hard body organisms. See Figures 1-1 and 1-7.

Darwinists also fail to explain the quantum increase of specified biological information necessary to account for the Cambrian Explosion of Animal life. Stephen Meyer [24] says, *"When you encounter the Cambrian Explosion with its huge and sudden appearance of radically new body plans, you realize an enormous amount of new biological information would have been necessary. The big question is, where did this information necessary to build compound eyes, complicated nervous systems, and articulated bodies come from? Darwinists don't have the answer. It's not even on their radar."* Modern biology does not support the Neo-Darwinian Interpretation even though they attempt to make you believe it does.

Punctuated Equilibrium Interpretation

Paleontologist Niles Eldridge,[25] Curator at the Smithsonian Institute, and the late paleontologist Stephen Jay Gould[25] advocated the Punctuated Equilibrium Interpretation. They wanted to come to terms with one of the most remarkable features of the fossil record which can be stated as follows: *"in any local area, species do not arise gradually by the steady transformation of its ancestors; species appear all at once fully formed. Most species exhibit stasis, that is, no directional morphological change during their tenure on earth. They appear in the fossil record much the same as when they disappear. They realized that morphological change is limited and directionless."*[26]

This Interpretation argues that once a new species appears, it proliferates into a large population and remains relatively unchanged for millions of years. Then a small number of individuals become isolated from the group and rapidly evolve into a new species leaving no trace of transitional forms in the fossil record. This idea is mystifying. It lacks scientific accuracy and credibility. However, it highly reinforces the idea that each new species appeared suddenly in the fossil record as a result of a special act of creation by the Creator of the Universe. See Figures 1-7 & 1-14.

Does the Fossil Record Support Punctuated Equilibrium?

Yes, the fossil record supports the Punctuated Equilibrium Interpretation in that all species always appear suddenly in the fossil record fully formed and during their time on Earth they experience stasis. But, this interpretation has failed to find **a scientific mechanism** to adequately explain the huge gaps that separate individual species or the big gap that separates the uniquely different body plans (phyla). For a lack of a mechanism, they have adopted the naturalistic **neo-Darwinian mechanism** to explain why evolution is the cause.

The Neo-Darwinian and the Punctuated Equilibrium Interpretations have the following points in common:

1. They both assume a fully naturalistic mechanism for universal descent.
2. They both embrace the idea that all new species arose as the product of an unguided, mechanistic, purposeless, naturalistic, chance process. All living organisms appear to be designed; however, they insist that such design is only apparent, not real.
3. They both share the idea that all organisms are related by common ancestry from an original single living organism. This would mean that blue green algae must have evolved from bacteria. This would be crossing the Kingdom Bridge. Would this be possible? Certainly not.
4. They both maintain that the only reality is to be found in the material portions of the universe. Do you see a flaw in this conclusion?
5. They both attempt to maintain religious neutrality in science. However, the followers for the most part are advocates of the religion of Naturalism and Humanism. Both interpretations deny the existence of God.

Intelligent Design Interpretation

Scientists who have conceived the Intelligent Design Interpretation have come to terms with the most remarkable features of the fossil record:

1. **That all species exhibit stasis, that implies no directional change during their tenure on earth.**
2. **Morphological change is usually limited and directionless.**
3. **In any local area, species do not arise gradually by the steady transformation of its ancestors. They appear suddenly in the fossil record fully formed (Figure 1-1).**

The Intelligent Design Interpretation is not based upon the Bible or any other Holy Book. **It is solely based upon scientific discoveries that reveal the presence of intelligent information within bio-systems.** A molecular analysis of living species within an information-theoretic framework reveals a vast amount of genetic information that points both to a prior intelligent cause as well as to long sequences of natural unintelligent causes. Biological information (e.g., DNA and proteins) implicates prior intelligent causes due to its specified complexity.

Again referring to Michael Behe [26] from Lehigh University in his book, *"Darwin's Black Box,"* where he discusses the biochemical complexity of a bacteria flagellum that is composed of at least three moving parts—a paddle, a rotor, and a motor. He describes the flagellum as being irreducibly complex. This means that it was impossible for it to have gradually evolved by the addition of different component parts slowly coming together. It had to have been designed and created intact because if even one component part of the flagellum becomes dysfunctional, then the entire bacteria becomes dysfunctional and dies.

Does the Fossil Record
Support Intelligent Design?

Yes, the Intelligent Design Interpretation is completely compatible with the fossil record. It is evident that the **Intelligent Designer is the cause or mechanism** for explaining why intelligent design is present in all bio-systems.

The Intelligent Design Interpretation does not identify the Intelligent Designer. Christians and Jews will identify the Intelligent Designer as the God of the Bible. Other persons will make their own identification of who the Intelligent Designer may be.

Surveys have shown that 80+% of persons in the United States and Canada believe there is a God. About 5 to 8% are atheists who believe there is no God. The in between group are agnostics who believe the existence of God is unknowable. The Intelligent Design Hypothesis would be relating to the 80+% of the people and to the in between group in a non threatening manner.

Why are Darwinian Evolutionists so frightened and so threatened by persons who believe in an All Powerful, All Knowing and Everywhere Present God? You will have to ask them.

Why Do Neo-Darwinists Hate Intelligent Design?

Atheistic Darwinists hate the Intelligent Design Interpretation because an Intelligent Designer or God is envisaged. They deny the very existence of God. On this basis they deny the very presence of intelligent design in all bio-systems. They maintain the intricate design that one witnesses in nature is only an apparent design. How can anyone believe this?

A Bible Based Interpretation

The Bible and geology are the basis for a Theistic Interpretation of the Cambrian Explosion of Animal life in this manuscript. Thanks to modern day science, the Bible record as it relates to science can now be scientifically trusted. It is now possible to show the remarkable relationship that exists between the Bible record and the scientific record of geology, paleontology, biology and all the natural sciences. See Figure 1-1.

This Interpretation addresses the remarkable feature of the fossil record that all species always appear suddenly in the fossil record fully formed. Each fossil exhibits stasis that is no directional change during their tenure on Earth. Morphological change is usually limited and directionless. The fossil record verifies that species do not arise gradually by the steady transformation of its ancestors. They appear suddenly and fully formed. This fact implies the work of an Intelligent Designer.

God's Plan for Animal Life

God always works everything according to a plan. We may ask the question, "Is there a hidden plan in this dramatic event called the Explosion of Animal Life?" Could this plan give added meaning to your life and mine? The answer is Yes.

God's original plan from the Lower Proterozoic to the present was to prepare the Earth, step by step, for the future habitation of Man. This plan is unveiled within the geologic column as revealed by the science of geology. See Figures 1-1 & 1-7.

The story of life on Earth is recorded in the fossil record. It begins at the beginning of the Proterozoic Age. The first species of bacteria and blue green chlorophyll generating algae (sea weeds and plankton) suddenly appeared. This is followed by many new species of bacteria and the more complex varieties of green algae and red and brown algae. God was in the process of developing a sophisticated food chain in preparation for the time when the first animal life would be formed and created.

God is the Origin of the Species

God truly is the source for the origin of the species. In reference to plant and animal life, God the Father is likened to the Master Architect or Intelligent Designer who designed all life. God the Son is likened to the Master Creator who created and formed all life; and God the Holy Spirit is likened to the Master Indweller or Heavenly Dove who broods as a mother hen, protecting, nourishing and giving warmth to all life. We read in John 1:4 (NIV), *"God is the source of all life."* He is the originator, author, designer, creator and sustainer of all life. See Figure 1-3.

It was at this point in time that we read this most remarkable phrase, *"And the Spirit of God was brooding over the waters of the Earth"* (Genesis 1:2). This is the first mention of God the Holy Spirit, who was at this early time, brooding as a mother hen over the waters of the earth giving warmth, protection and nourishment to the life that was now in the process of being created by the Divine Creator, the Lord Jesus Christ in the ocean waters throughout the Earth. This was all accomplished by carrying out the architectural plan set out by the Divine Architect, God the Father.

We read in John 1:1-5 (NIV), *"¹In the beginning was the Word, and the Word was with God, and the Word was God. ²He was with God in the beginning. ³Through him all things were made; without him nothing was made that has been made. ⁴In him was life and that life was the light of all mankind. ⁵The light shines in the darkness, and the darkness has not overcome it."* We then read in John 1:14, (NIV) *"¹⁴The Word became flesh and made his dwelling among us. We have seen his glory, the glory of the one and only Son, who came from the Father, full of grace and truth."* These two portions of scripture clearly identify the Word as no other than Jesus Christ who is the Creator of the universe, the Earth and of all life. See Figure 1-3.

God is the source of all life. We can we truthfully say that God is a scientist extraordinary? In the Bible God is pictured as a "Super-Scientist."

First Appearance of Animal Life

Four animal species were created by God towards the end of the Proterozoic Age. They were a sponge, a jelly fish, a type of worm and a trace of a shelly type of animal. These animal species represented four different Phyla.

During the dramatic Cambrian Explosion of Animal Life about 40+ additional Phyla suddenly appeared in what geologists refer to as a geologic instant. Then, at the end of the Cambrian Age, the first major extinction of animal life took place. From that time onward, only about 35 or so Phyla have continued to the present. See Figure 1-1.

How God Created Animal Species

The method God used to plan, create and form the human species is believed to be the same method He used to plan, create and form every animal species, male and female, on Earth. God the Father, the Master Architect of the universe is the one who outlined a detailed architectural blueprint for each animal species, male and female, and the exact time when each species would be created and formed on Earth by the Creator, the Lord Jesus Christ. The male would have been created first, than the female. This creative act would ensure that the male and female of each species would be genetically related. They would then be capable of reproducing fertile offspring from generation to generation. Each animal species has been created to fulfill a definite ecological God-given plan and purpose under the protection and direction of the Heavenly Dove, God the Holy Spirit for this Earth. See Figure 1-3 and 1-15.

The Four Hebrew Words

There are four Hebrew words that describe how God planned, created and formed all things. They are Kun, Bara, Yatsar and Asah (Figure 1-15).

Figure 1-15: The four Hebrew words that reveal how God Planned, Created, Formed and Made all Creation

Kun means to come forth with an architectural blueprint or plan for each species of life that is so perfect that no future alterations are necessary. Kun is another name for God the Father, the Master Intelligent Designer and Architect who came forth with a plan for all life. He planned every detail that pertains to every species of bacteria, viral, plant and animal life and also for the future arrival of Man. God the Father delegated all the work of creating all life to God the Son, the Master Creator, who created and formed each species of bacteria, viral, animal and plant life according to that plan. See Figures 1-15 and 1-3.

Bara when used as a noun means the Creator Himself. Isaiah 40:28 (NKJV) says, *"Have you not known? Have you not heard? The everlasting God, the Lord, the Creator (Bara)* *of the ends of the earth, neither faints nor is weary. There is no searching of His understanding."* Bara when used as a verb has two primary meanings. It means the Creator has the power to create something new out of nothing. Secondly, it means that the Creator has the power to create something new out of previous existing matter and the end result is just as great as if He had created it out of nothing. Bara always implies original creation. Whenever a new species was created by the Creator, Bara means that this species was never in existence prior to this moment in time. The fossil record confirms that each species of plant, animal, viral and bacteria appear suddenly in the fossil record fully formed and with no ancestors.

Yatsar means to form something new out of previously existing matter. It is a process that implies the work of a Master Potter who is forming a beautiful vase out of clay. For example, when God created the human species, the Creator, the Lord Jesus Christ knelt down and formed (yatsar) the body of Adam out of previously existing dead clay particles. He then created (bara) life within Adam's body by breathing into his nostrils the breath of life and Adam became the first living human being on Earth. God then put Adam into a deep sleep. He removed a rib from Adam and made (asah) Eve. In this rib was all the necessary genetic information necessary to make woman. In this miraculous process, God genetically related Adam to Eve so that they would be of the same species capable of reproducing fertile offspring after their kind. Likewise, God genetically related each male and female species of life from Day One to the present, so that they could propagate offspring from generation to generation.

We read an interesting confirmation of how we are all fearfully and wonderfully made in Psalm 139: 13-18 NIV which says, *"13For you created my inmost being; you knit me together in my mother's womb. 14I praise you because I am fearfully and wonderfully made; your works are wonderful, I know that full well. 15 My frame was not hidden from you when I was made in the secret place, when I was woven together in the depths of the earth. 16Your eyes saw my unformed body; all the days ordained for me were written in your book before one of them came to be. 17How precious to me are your thoughts, God! How vast is the sum of them! 18Were I to count them, they would outnumber the grains of sand when I awake, I am still with you."* The science of micro or molecular biology confirms the accuracy of the above description of life within all livings cells so that they are able to propagate offspring from generation to generation.

Science refers to man as a species called Homo sapiens. The science of geology now confirms that Man and woman appeared during the latter portion of the Pleistocene Ice Age or more specifically during the geological Anathermal Age. To find the details see Volume Two by H. Donald Daae. 27

Asah has a general meaning that is often translated as made. It has great latitude, but never to indicate original creation. Asah can be simply illustrated by observing a twelve year old boy that God has made (asah). Asah implies that there was a time when this boy experienced creation (bara) at conception. This boy was never in existence prior to this point in time. From the moment of conception to the present, God has been forming (yatsar) that boy. You are now observing a twelve year old boy that God has made (asah). However, the process of yatsar will continue until this boy will one day grow old and die.

The Bible gives specific information about how God created, formed and made each species of animal life. The Bible portrays God as a super scientist extra-ordinary. In order for God to have created all animal life, He had to be a super molecular biologist and bio-chemist, and the list could go on and on. Science now confirms that the Bible is scientifically correct. **It gives a logical explanation for the Origin of**

the Species. In this scenario, an All Mighty, All Powerful, All Knowing God is the scientific source for every species of animal life and of Man on Earth. For additional information see APPENDIX D.

The Cambrian Explosion of Animal Life is Important

The Cambrian Explosion of Animal Life is important because every species of animal life from the Cambrian Period to the present belongs to one of the 35 or so animal Phyla that survived the Cambrian Period. This event applies to all the micro and macro sized species of animal life.

For instance, the Chordate Phylum is characterized by having a vertebral column with a notochord. All vertebrate animal life belongs to this phylum. This has nothing to do with evolution, but has everything to do with God's Master Plan.

Truly the Cambrian Explosion of Animal life has set the stage for the next five Creation Days. Every new species of animal life from this time to the present relate directly to one of the 35 or so Phyla that God created during the Cambrian Explosion of Animal Life. Let us now explore the fascinating events of Day Two.

Concluding Remarks

The following events took place during the First Creation Day:

1. God planned, created, formed and made the vast universe of stars and galaxies. According to astronomers this event took place at least 14+ billion years into the past.
2. God created, formed and made the Earth about 4.6+ billion years ago. See Figures 1-1 and 1-7.

3. God created, formed and made a beautiful and magnificent Primordial, Garden called Eden that encompassed the entire Earth at the beginning of the geological Archean Age. See Figure 1-7.

4. This magnificent garden was decked with beautiful gemstones. It became the home for Lucifer and hosts of angels under his supervision.

5. At the end of an 800 million year period, the greatest tragedy of tragedies took place when sin was found in the heart of Lucifer. He at this time lured many of his angels into a life of sin and open rebellion against the God of heaven and Earth. As a result, the Earth became a dark, sin cursed planet from this time forward to the present. This tragic event terminated the geological Archean Age.

6. God then ushered in the Proterozoic Age. The beginning of the Proterozoic Age is marked by the dramatic birth of the oceans with the sudden appearance of bacteria and algae species and the deposit of the first water laid sediments on Earth.

7. Towards the end of the Proterozoic Age, God created four marine species of animal life that relate to four separate phyla.

8. During the Lower Cambrian Age, God established a plan for all future animal life including Man. this event is called, **"The Cambrian Explosion of Animal Life."** God created 40+ phyla. Each phylum had a unique body plan. At the end of the Cambrian Period, the surviving Phyla were reduced to about 35. Every species of animal life, micro and macro, that God created since that time can be placed into one of these 35 or so body plans called a phyla. Throughout geological history of the Earth, God has created a great variety of additional species of marine and land plant life so that the future animal life would have adequate food and sustenance. To see how this plan unfolds, it is necessary to read the following five chapters.

References for Chapter One

1. Random House, Webster's College Dictionary, December 3, 1990.
2. Dr. Roger C Wiens, "Radiometric Dating A Christian Perspective." See rwiens@prodigy.net. www.http://asa.calvin.edu/ASA/resource/weins.com.
3. Walter J. Beasley, F.R.G.S., *"Creation's Amazing Architect," London by Marshall, Morgan & Scott. 1955.* p.35 on p.20
4. Alexander Cruden, "Cruden's Unabridged Concordance," Fleming H. Revell Company. 14th Printing, Westwood, New Jersey, London, Glascow. 1965. p.224.
5. Special Edition of Scientific American, "Our Ever Changing Earth," Volum 15, Number 2, 2005, published by Scientific American., Inc., 415 madison Avenue, New York, NY 10017.
6. David A Lindsey, "Glacial Sedimentology of the Precambrian Gowganda Formation, Ontario, Canada." Author Affiliations, U.S Geological Survey, Denver, Colorado. This article was found on Google.
7. Bargoorn Elso, "The Oldest Fossils." Scientific American, August 1963.
8. Max D. Rittenden, Jr., Nichola Christie Buck and Paul Karl Link, "Evidence for two Pulses of Glaciation during the Late Proterozoic in Northern Utah and Southeastern Idaho." This was from Google.
9. Gould, Stephen Jay, "Wonderful Life: The Burgess Shale and the Nature of History," W.W. Norton & Company, N.Y., London, 1990,. 59. p.p.69—76.
10. Simon Conway Morris, "The Crucible of Creation," Oxford University Press, Oxford, New York, Melbourne, p. 169.
11. Fred Heeren, "The Cosmic Pursuit Magazine, The Day Star Network. A Report on the Proceedings of the International Symposium at Chengjiang, in China, June & July of 1999. p.19.

12. Gould, ibid aa. p.59.
13. Hereen P.20.
14. Paul Chien PhD. Personal communication re: Prof. J.Y. Chen's explanation of the depositional history of the Burgess Fossils in China.
15. Murray Coopold & Wayne Powell, "A Geoscience Guide to The Burgess Shale" page 18. Produced by the Yoho-Burgess Shale Foundation in 2000. copies can be obtained at www.burgess-shale.bc.ca. or e-mail www.burgshal@rockies.net.
16. Copold & Powell, p. 18.
17. Copold & Powell, p. 18.
18. Copold & Powell, p. 27.
19. Copold & Powell, P. 27.
20. Coppold & Powell, p. 28.
21. Gould, as above, p.76.
22. Behe, Michael, "Darwin's Black Box," The Free Press, NY, London, Toronto, 1996, Ch.3, p.72.
23. Behe, Michael J., "Darwin's Black Box," The Free Press, NY, London, Toronto, 1996,
24. Behe, Michael J., "Darwin's Black Box," The Free Press, NY, London, Toronto, 1996, p.39.
25. Stephen Meyer, "The Origin of Biological Information and the Higher Taxonomic Categories." Proceedings from the Biological Society of Washington, Sept. 15, 2004. Also find at www.discovery.org/scripts/viewDB/index.php?command=view&id=2177.
26. N. Eldridge and Stephen J. Gould, 1972, "Punctuated Equilibria: An Alternative to Phyletic Gradualism." In T.J.M. Models in Paleobiology, p.82-115, San Francisco: Freeman, Cooper & Company.
27. Behe, Michael J., "Darwin's Black Box," The Free Press, NY, London, Toronto, 1996, p.72.
28. Daae H. Donald. "Bridging The Gap, The 7th Day: Who Was Early Man, Age of Phenomenal Accomplishments" Vol. Two.

Chapter 2

The Second Day of Creation

The Bible Record

The Second Day of Creation is recorded in Genesis 1:6-8 (NKJV) as follows, *"⁶Then God said, "Let there be a firmament in the midst of the waters, and let it divide the waters from the waters." ⁷Thus God made the firmament, and divided the waters which were under the firmament from the waters which were above the firmament; and it was so. ⁸ And God called the firmament Heaven. So the evening and the morning were the second day."*

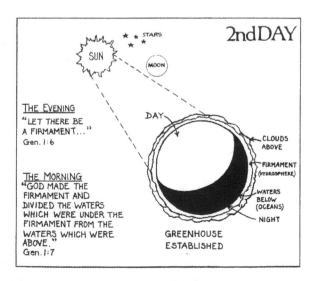

Figure 2-1: An Illustration of the Biblical Second Day of Creation.

The Bible record indicates that certain fundamental transformations took place upon the Earth during the Second Day of Creation which resulted in world-wide changes in climate. These fundamental changes had a direct impact upon the Earth's hydrosphere. In other words, God was now blanketing the Earth with a layer of clouds. This of course had a direct impact upon the Earth's climate.

A Greenhouse Effect Established

The result of these changes is assumed to be an increase in the effect of the Earth's atmosphere to trap heat from the sun. God was generating a thick moist cloud cover in the upper hydrosphere. This contributed to a rise in temperature and humidity producing a "**Greenhouse Effect**."

This increased heat and moisture resulted in warmer temperatures throughout the Earth. It produced an environment well-suited to marine plant and animal life. The suggestion here is that God enhanced the environment to contribute to the rapid growth and prosperity of the marine flora and fauna of this geological period.

More specifically, these above passages describe a creative process whereby God was in the process of blanketing the Earth with a garment of clouds. He divided the waters which were above the firmament from the waters below. The waters above were clouds; the waters below were the ocean waters. The system as a whole is referred to as the hydrosphere. The hydrosphere consists of three main components, the liquid water on the Earth's surface, moisture-bearing air, and dense accumulations of water vapor in the form of clouds. The hydrosphere is, as a result, often associated with the sustenance and maintenance of life on Earth.

The word firmament, which we here relate to the hydrosphere, is *raqiya* in Hebrew, meaning to "stamp out," or to "spread out by striking." This usage appears more graphically in

Isaiah 40:22 (NKJV) *"It is I that stretches out the heavens as a curtain, and spreads them out like a tent, within which life dwells."*

The single greatest significance of the separation of the firmament was, in fact, the resulting increased suitability of the Earth as a habitat for future terrestrial plants and animals. The cloud layer would have provided an effective set of environmental controls for warmer temperature, moisture and lighting. Up to this point in time and throughout the Second Day, there are no indications of terrestrial plant or animal life as yet anywhere throughout the Earth.

The key word in Genesis 1:7 is the Hebrew word *asah*, translated as "made." This Hebrew word "asah" does not denote primary creation; rather it presupposes existing things being manipulated into new forms. The meaning, then, is that the hydrosphere or firmament had been in existence prior to the Second Day. Secondly, it implies that the hydrosphere had already been formed (*yatsar*), and it was now being given a new appointment or assignment during the Second Day. See Figure 1-14.

It is implicit to realize that water existed prior to the Second Day. Firstly, the description is of the separation of the waters; and secondly references to water on the newly created Earth appear much earlier during the First Creation Day. In Genesis 1:2 (NKJV) we read *"And the Spirit of God moved upon the face of the waters."* The previous existence of water implies an existing "water cycle" was already in existence.

This water cycle was established when the "Birth of the Oceans" took place during the First Creation Day. See Figure 1-11. However, during the Second Day dramatic changes took place in the hydrosphere, whereby a layer of moist clouds, referred to as the "waters above," were separated from the "waters below" creating a greenhouse effect. See Figure 2-1.

The Evening and the Morning

The Second Day began with a plan and ended with the consummation of that plan. The planning stage, or the evening of the Second Day, is stated as follows: *"And God said, let there be a firmament" (Genesis 1:6, NKJV))*. This was the plan conceived in the mind of the Great Divine Architect in the evening of this Second Day.

The working stage commenced in the morning and was completed during the day time as follows, *"And God made the firmament"* (Genesis 1:7, NKJV). The word "made" is the Hebrew word *asah*, which implies that the work had now been completed and that the Amazing Creator had now carried out the plan of his Father the Great Divine Architect. A summary of the planning and working stages of this day is as follows: "And the EVENING and the MORNING were the Second Day" (Genesis 1:8). See Appendix C for clarification.

The Second Day ended with fundamental changes in the nature of the hydrosphere. This resulted in the establishment of a fully-developed greenhouse effect upon the Earth.

The Geological Record of the 2nd Day

The geological portion of time corresponding to the Second Day relates to the geological Ordovician Age. It extends to the end of the Middle Silurian Age, a period of about 100 million years, geologically speaking. See Figure 1-1.

A considerable length of time is evident in the rocks of the Second Day. In the deeper sedimentary basin regions of North America, the accumulated thicknesses of this age are locally in excess of 11,000 feet (3,352.8m). I have had the privilege of observing and mapping these sediments in the north/south trending Richardson Mountain basinal region of the northern Yukon Territories of Canada. In the

Canadian Arctic Islands, these same age basinal sediments and associated carbonate bank edges are regionally in the range of 20,000+ feet (6,096+m) in thickness. These great thicknesses of sediments extend for great distances.

The great variance in thickness of the sedimentary units of the First and Second Days is illustrated in Figure 2-2. The rock units are shown to thicken and thin from the Deep Water Basin regions to the more shallow water platform regions of the North American continent.

On the basis of geology, it would appear that the continental regions of the Earth were submerged by water for the major portion of this age to the end of the Middle Silurian Period when a big change took place.

During the Upper Silurian Age, the North American continent experienced uplift and orogenic mountain building. This is known geologically as the Taconic Orogeny. This allowed major portions of the Earth to rise above sea level. As a result, the sediments of Upper Silurian Age must be considered to be a part of the Third Creation Day.

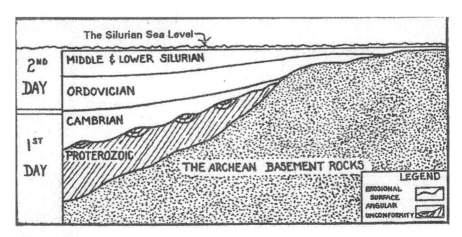

Figure 2-2: Relates the Second Day of Creation to the Geological Record of the Ordovician and the Lower and Middle Silurian Ages.

Climate of the 2nd Day

The geological sciences provide evidences to substantiate that a strong greenhouse effect was in place throughout the Earth during the entire Ordovician Age except for a fairly brief time during the Upper Ordovician Age. The greenhouse continued throughout the Lower and Middle Silurian Ages. See Figure 1-1.

An important indicator of these climate changes in the geological record is the rise and fall of sea water levels. The progress of the waters surrounding and / or overlying the North American continent is a typical example. What we observe, in general, are two things. Firstly, that during the Ordovician and Silurian Periods there were significant fluctuations in the level of the oceans tending towards the near or complete submergence of the continents throughout the Lower and Middle Silurian ages, and secondly, a corresponding warming of the Earth's surface.

Fluctuations in sea level always have a global impact, and these significant changes in the elevation of the sea surrounding North America had an equally significant effect on all the other continental regions throughout the world.

A faunal (fossil) break at the end of the Cambrian marks the distinct difference between the Cambrian and the overlying Ordovician sediments. This is based upon the sudden appearance of many new species of marine animal life. Persons who are specialists in invertebrate paleontology are now able to differentiate the sediments of the underlying Cambrian formations from the overlying Ordovician sediments.

First Greenhouse Established

The beginning of the Ordovician witnessed a great spreading or advance of the seas over the land. This is often referred to as the "Great Submergence." At least half of North America was under water, and the remaining platform areas were reduced to a series of broad, low islands. This condition persisted throughout the Ordovician, except for a local north-south trending uplift (called the *Taconian Orogeny*) along the eastern coastal region of North America. This local uplift began during the Middle Ordovician and continued to the beginning of the Silurian.

During the Lower and Middle Ordovician, the climate appeared to be relatively warm and uniform without well-defined climate zones. Clark and Stearn[1] describe this period as follows, "*Climate zones which roughly follow lines of latitude may not have been as well differentiated in Ordovician time as they are at present, so that the temperature of the Epeiric Sea would have been approximately the same at latitude 35°N as at 70°N. This is difficult to reconcile with what we know of the present condition of the ocean. A strong warm current, such as the Gulf Stream, might have kept the marine environment of the Epeiric Sea uniformly warm even in the north. This hypothesis cannot be tested, however, for we know of no comparable modern epeiric seas in which such currents might be found.*"

The warm, uniform temperatures of the waters can be explained by a greenhouse effect that was firmly in place by Lower and Middle Ordovician time because there appears to be a lack of variable climate zones.

The Upper Ordovician Ice Age

Geology confirms that the climate became somewhat cooler during the Upper Ordovician, as evidenced by Glaciation in different parts of the Earth. Glacial ice covered thousands of square miles in the central Sahara region of northern Africa. The Upper Ordovician rocks of this age confirm that great glacial striations can be followed for many miles. Also the magnificent outwash plains with fluvial-glacial channels, eskers, drumlins, etc. are all earmarks of a giant continental Glaciation. See Figures 1-1 and 2-3.

Evidences of this Ice Age are also present in rocks of the same age in the eastern part of Brazil. It is believed that North and South America were attached to Europe and Africa at this time. It is possible that the cooler climate would have had a certain impact on other regions of the Earth during the Upper Ordovician. However, I am not aware of glacial ice being present in any other parts of the Earth during the Upper Ordovician.

Two conditions are necessary for the formation of ice, namely an abundant supply of precipitation and a pronounced cooling of the climate. A break in the greenhouse effect during the Upper Ordovician Age could satisfy these two requirements. This would have resulted in great amounts of water to have been released in the form of precipitation. The clearing of the skies would have resulted in a lowering of the temperature, thus causing snow and ice to accumulate in parts of the Earth that were above sea level.

It is herein believed that the purpose of this Ice Age was to rejuvenate the Earth's climate in preparation for the creation of new life that would lead to a new geological Age called the Silurian Period. See Figure 1-1.

Second Greenhouse

The close of the Upper Ordovician Age in North America saw a narrow band of rugged mountains in Appalachia, whereas the remainder of the continent continued to be low-lying. It is believed that the sea retreated and much of the continent was above sea level for a short time.

The Early Silurian Period saw a great spreading of the seas, such that by Middle Silurian time most of the continental regions were covered by water once again. This included portions of the Appalachian Mountain region, which, over several millions of years, had eroded to a lower stature.

During the Early Silurian, there is also evidence of a significant warming of the climate. This was a result of the increasing cloud coverage and the re-establishment of the Greenhouse Effect.

The warm climate of the Silurian Period has been described by Dunbar and Waage[2] as follows, "*Except for the Appalachian geosyncline, all these seas must have been warm, clear and shallow, since the Silurian deposits are almost exclusively limestone and abound in corals that built reefs in many places, from Tennessee across Kentucky and Indiana and along the west side of the Hudson Bay and in the Lake Winnipeg region of Canada. Some of the Silurian reefs in northern Indiana were as much as a mile across and 75 feet thick.*"

Coral reefs that were thriving in the northern latitudes of Arctic Canada at that time were similar to those thriving in more southerly regions. This implies that the climate was warm throughout the Earth during the Silurian Period without the well-defined warm and cold regions which exist today.

Geology confirms that reef development during this age was phenomenal. For instance, the company I used to work with participated in the drilling of a well on Banks Island in the High Arctic regions of Canada. This well encountered a Silurian pinnacle reef that was over 4,000 feet (1219.2 meters) in height. It rose above the underlying carbonate platform of Lower Silurian and Ordovician age.

The total Silurian and Ordovician Carbonate and basinal shale sediments of this age are often in the 10,000 to 20,000 foot (3048-6086 meters) range in thickness throughout much of the High Arctic of Canada. I have had the privilege of mapping the regional Ordovician / Silurian Formations throughout the NWT region and later was able to extend my mapping of these rock units through the northern (NWT) regions of Canada and the Northern Yukon and then westward through the central and northern portions of Alaska.

The uniform warm temperatures during the Lower and Middle Silurian can be explained by the re-establishment of the greenhouse effect.

Ordovician & Silurian Life

The Bible is silent as to the type of life God created during the Second Day. However, the following principle applies, *"When the Bible is silent, the Earth speaks."* Geology, through the science of paleontology, is able to describe the species of marine invertebrate animal life that were created during the Second Day.

It is important to note that the marine plant life in the form of algae, sea weeds and bacteria that were present throughout the previous First Day continued to flourish throughout the Second Day. Food and nourishment were thus provided for the many newly created species of invertebrate animal life that were unique and different from the previous Cambrian Age.

Dunbar & Waage[3] say, "*The faunal break at the end of the Cambrian Period indicates that the continent was completely emergent for a time, but the Late Cambrian lands were low and in North America the period closed quietly. The post Cambrian hiatus apparently reflects a gentle drop in sea level. But with the beginning of Ordovician time another great cycle of submergence began as shallow epicontinental seas swept in from the east, west, north and south. Early in the period the Appalachian trough and much of the eastern half of the United States were flooded and an extensive sea spread across northern Canada while another covered parts of California, Nevada, Utah, Wyoming and Colorado. Later in the period fully half of the continent was submerged and the land was reduced to a series of great low islands. No later submergences was quite so extensive."* They go on to say, *"The Lower Ordovician formations are all calcareous— limestone's or dolostone's—indicating that all the land surfaces were so low that they suffered little erosion."*

During the Lower Ordovician Period the seas widely spread across all of the USA and Canada. This included the Canadian Shield and the High Arctic regions as well as all land regions throughout the Earth.

New Animal Life

Dunbar and Waage relate that many new species of marine invertebrate animal life appeared at different periods of time during the Second Creation Day. It must be remembered that when the dramatic Lower Cambrian Explosion of Animal Life took place about 40+ animal phyla were represented by species that were unique to the Cambrian Age. However, at the end of the Cambrian Period it would appear that the number of phyla was reduced to about 35 or so. Persons who specialize in paleontology would be able to identify which species relate to the Cambrian Age and which ones are new. We will now investigate some of the major phyla of this age. See Figures 2-3 & 1-1.

Phylum Arthropod: Dunbar and Waage[4] say, *"Trilobite species probably reached their peak in variety and numbers during Early Ordovician time. Many new species quite different from those of the Cambrian suddenly appeared at different times during the long Ordovician and Silurian Epochs. Later during this period and following periods of time, the trilobites began a great decline which continued until their extinction shortly before the end of the Paleozoic Era."* Trilobites belong to the Arthropod Phylum.

Phylum Brachiopod: Dunbar and Waage[5] say, "*Brachiopods in Cambrian time were small and nearly all bore thin chitin type shells. Chitin is a nitrogenous substance similar to fingernails. Many new species of brachiopods appeared during the Ordovician. Nearly all of them bore limy type shells. They were the dominant "invertebrate life" of this time.*" The question arises, did these new species that belong to the Brachiopod Phylum evolve or were they individually created by the Great Divine Creator. It is interesting to note that each species appeared suddenly, fully formed without any ancestors. Each new species continued to reproduce offspring after their kind during this 70+ million year period. There are no evidences of one brachiopod species evolving into another brachiopod species.

Phylum Bryozoans: Dunbar and Waage say,[6] "*Bryozoa are represented by four distinct orders and a host of new genera and species. Many of the limestone and limy shale intervals of strata contain a record of these bryozoans. They and the brachiopods are by far the most abundant Ordovician fossils.*"

Phylum Mollusca: Dunbar & Waage[7] say, "*Of the great phylum Mollusca only the gastropods (snails) were represented in the Cambrian and these were quite small and of two kinds; but early in Ordovician time they appeared in great numbers and bewildering variety, some with low, spired shells and others with slender, graceful spires of many whorls. By Middle Ordovician time one genus (Maclurites) were making shells as much as 8 inches across.*"

Dunbar & Waage[8] also say, "*Cephalopods were exceedingly rare and quite small in the latest Cambrian but, near the base of the Ordovician, nautiloid cephalopods appeared in abundance and many of these had rather specialized shells. One tribe in the early Ordovician developed shells larger than that of the modern Nautilus and by the middle of the period one of the straight-shelled tribes, the endoceroids, produced shells as much as 15 feet long and over ten inches in diameter at the living chamber. This was the largest animal on earth during the Ordovician."* Cephalopods belong to the Mollusca Phylum.

THE BIBLICAL RECORD		THE GEOLOGICAL RECORD			INTERPERTATION
		Period	Evidence	Stratigraphy	
The 3rd Day	*"Let the dry land appear"*: Gen. 1:9	Silurian U 400M yr.	Caledonian Orogoney	Regional Erosion & Uplift	
The 2nd Day	*"God made the firmament and divided the water above from the waters below."* Gen. 1:6 cloud cover Greenhouse established	Silurian M L	Support for Greenhouse		There were many separate acts of Special Creation throughout the 2nd Day
		Ordo- vician U M L 500M yr.	Ice Age --?-- Support for Greenhouse		
The 1st Day		Camb- rian U M L		Shelf Basinal Carbonates Shales	

Figure 2-3: The sediments of the 2nd Day of Creation are shown as they relate to the Arctic Islands region and to northern Yukon and Alaska. These shallow water carbonate sediments are found in continental regions and the basinal shales are found in deeper water regions throughout the Earth. Fossil assemblages are similar worldwide. Compare with Figure 1-1. Original prepared by Don Daae.

Dunbar & Waage[9] further state, *"The Pelecypods (clams) made their appearance near the base of the Middle Ordovician, and this first fauna had thin and small shells little more than an inch long, but later in the period, larger shells in considerable variety developed."*

Phylum Coelenterata: Dunbar & Waage[10] say, *"Corals, totally unknown in the Cambrian, are represented by two distinct orders near the base of the Middle Ordovician. One of these belongs to the Rugosa or "horn corals" and the other to the Tabulata. The earliest of the latter (Tetradium) were colonial forms with minute, slender, four-sided corallites,* *but soon were joined by the first of the honeycomb corals (Favosites), and the chain corals (Halysites), The oldest known coral reefs were made by Lamottia, a primitive relative of the "honeycombs" in the Middle Ordovician."* These corals were dominant in the growth of reefs. Many of these coral reefs were of giant proportions.

Phylum Echinodermata: Dunbar & Waage[11] say, *"The great Phylum Echinodermata was represented by only a few kinds in Cambrian time. But, near the base of the Lower Ordovician starfish and brittle stars appear and before the end of the period some of the starfish closely resembled small modern species that feed on the oyster beds along the U.S. Atlantic coast. In the Mid-Ordovician in Scotland the oldest true sea urchin (echinoderm) was found. Small crinoids of many distinct species are also found in Ordovician rocks."*

Phylum Crustacean: Dunbar & Waage[12] say, *"The Crustacean Phylum are represented by several groups, notably the Ostracoda Group, whose bean-shaped bivalve shells in places almost cover the bedding planes. Ostracods are still present in the modern seas where they are an important source of food for the larger animals."*

Subphylum Hemichordate: Dunbar & Waage[13] say, *"The **Graptolites**, which are so abundant in the dark grey to black shales, deserve note because they were mostly floaters, drifting like the sargassum does in the modern oceans, and thus spread rapidly to far places. They are thus one of the most important fossils for intercontinental correlation. They evolved rapidly during Ordovician time and mark a number of faunal zones that can be recognized in both the eastern and western zones that can be recognized in north America and in Europe and even in far-off Australia."*

The First Fish

The Agnatha are often categorized as "jawless fish." They are found in rocks of late Ordovician age. They became numerous during the following Silurian and Devonian ages, and then became extinct at the beginning of the Carboniferous. However, true fish with a true bony vertical column had not yet arrived on Earth.

Most Agnatha were small, less than one foot in length, and nearly all were covered with a tough coat of bony plates. They had no obvious internal skeleton. However, they may have had an un-calcified organic cartilage that was not preserved. For all practical purposes, they should be classified with the invertebrates. They are considered a fish in the current literature because of their fish-like appearance.

New Invertebrate Life

During the Second Day God created many new species of invertebrate animal life and the strange Agnatha fish-like species. These many new species always appeared suddenly at different intervals of time during the Ordovician and the Lower and Middle Silurian Ages. As a result, scientists called paleontologists are able to determine whether the sediments are of Lower, Middle or Upper Ordovician Age or of Lower and Middle Silurian Age.

In other words each successive age has new unique fossil assemblages. Each fossil species is unique and different because they were individually planned by the Amazing Architect and created by the Amazing Creator. See Figures 1-3 and 1-14. There are no evidences of one species actually slowly evolving into a new species as the Darwinian Theory would have us believe. Whether you want to believe that God did it or that evolution did it is up to the reader.

Each of the above mentioned species of invertebrate animal life relate directly to one of the 35 or so body plans called phyla that God created and established during the Lower Cambrian Explosion of Animal life. Also all of these new species are unique to this geological age worldwide.

Marine Plant life

There are no direct evidences of land plants being present on the Earth up to this point in time. However, the many species of algae that are found in abundance throughout the previous Proterozoic and Cambrian Ages provided the food for the Ordovician and the Silurian animal life.

The evidence of the Bible record is that God was in the process of preparing the Earth as a suitable environment for the arrival of land plants and land animals. The two successive periods of enhanced heat and moisture referred to as "Greenhouse Effects" bear witness to this fact.

We may ask the question, are these sediments of the 2nd Day the product of Noah's Flood as Creation Science People believe? Definitely not. Is this the product of Evolution? Definitely not. Evolution isn't competent enough to accomplish this enormous, intelligent and well planned task. But our Creator is able. He is All Powerful, All Knowing and Everywhere Present. He is the One who was capable of planning, designing, forming and making the Second Day of Creation to become a reality on a worldwide scale. He is the One who created new species of animal life that are unique in their design to any other age before and after. This is the reason, why paleontologists are ever thankful and are able to confidently identify this age as being different and unique from any other geological age before or after.

The science of geology gives an insight into God's creative plan for the Second Creation Day. Sediments of this age were regionally deposited systematically and geologists are able to map them on every continent throughout the Earth. Truly, this was the design of an Omnipotent, Omniscient and Omnipresent God.

Each of the species of animal life that one finds in sediments of the Second Day reveal that each species lived for a brief period of time and then died. The question arises, why did they die? It was because of the Fall of Lucifer during the First Creation Day that left a black curse of death upon the Earth. This is the result of "The Edenic Curse."

Concluding Remarks

During the Second Day of Creation God created and formed literally hundreds of new invertebrate species of animal life. As was mentioned earlier, each new species can be placed into a definite Phyla or Body Plan. See Figure 1-12.

Each of these species of invertebrate animal life relates directly to one of the 35 or so phyla that God created and established during the Cambrian Explosion of Animal life. Also each of these species are unique to this geological age worldwide.

In other words each successive geological age have new unique fossil assemblages. Each new fossil species is unique and different from any previous species because they were each individually planned by the Amazing Architect and were created as unique by the Amazing Creator. There are no evidences of one species slowly evolving into another new species as the Darwinian Theory would have us believe. Whether you want to believe that God did it or that evolution did it is up to the reader to decide.

It is interesting to note that each of the Six Days of Creation ends with the phrase where God said, "It was good," except for the Second Day. **There is a certain mystery as to why God could not say that the Second Day was good.** In order to find the most plausible answer, it is necessary to find it in the accompanying Volume by H. Donald Daae.[14]

References for the Second Day

1. Clark and Stearn, "Geological Evolution of North America," Second Edition, 1968, The Ronald Press Company, USA p. 146.
2. Carl O. Dunbar and Karl M. Waage, *Historical Geology*, Third Edition (New York: John Wiley and Sons, Inc., 1969, p. 215.
3. Dunbar & Waage, p.190 & 191
4. Dunbar & Waage, p.206
5. Dunbar & Waage, p.206
6. Dunbar & Waage, p.206
7. Dunbar & Waage, p.206
8. Dunbar & Waage, p.206
9. Dunbar & Waage, p.206
10. Dunbar & Waage, p.206
11. Dunbar & Waage, p.206
12. Dunbar & Waage, p.207
13. Dunbar & Waage, p.207
14. Daae H. Donald, "Bridging The Gap, The 7th Day Who Was Early Man—Vol.2, Age of Phenomenal Accomplishments."

Chapter 3

The Third Day of Creation

Introduction

Through the course of the Second Day, with its profound changes in climate, the Earth was being conditioned and prepared for the first appearance of land plants and new land and water animal life. It is interesting to note that the Greenhouse Effect of the Second Day continued to prevail throughout the Third Day of Creation.

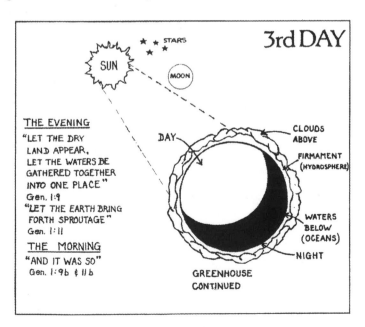

Figure 3-1: The Biblical Third Day of Creation

Until the beginning of the Third Day, only marine plant and marine animal life were present on the Earth. The first distinct "Land Plants" appeared during the Upper Silurian Period, which equates to the beginning of the Third Creation Day. As a whole, the Third Day corresponds to the geological Upper Silurian, Devonian, Mississippian and Pennsylvanian Periods. This age extends from about 280 to 400 million years before the present based upon geological and radiometric dating methods. This is a span of about 120 million years. See Figure 1-1.

The Bible Record

The Third Day of Creation is recorded in Genesis 1:9-13 (NIV) 9And God said, "*Let the water under the sky be gathered to one place, and let dry ground appear." And it was so. 10God called the dry ground "land," and the gathered waters he called "seas." And God saw that it was good. 11Then God said, "Let the land produce vegetation: seed-bearing plants and trees on the land that bear fruit with seed in it, according to their various kinds." And it was so. 12 The land produced vegetation: plants bearing seed according to their kinds and trees bearing fruit with seed in it according to their kinds. And God saw that it was good. 13And there was evening, and there was morning—the third day.*"

The Third Day of Creation is divided into an evening and a morning. It was in the evening that God the Father came forth with an architectural blueprint or plan for this day. It was in the morning and throughout this day that the Creator performed the work necessary to bring this Third Day into fruition or reality. See Figures 3-1 and 1-1,

The plan in verse 9 envisages that the Earth at the beginning of the Third Day was completely covered or submerged by sea water. It was at this time that the **land began to emerge** above sea level. The Third Day envisages that all the water would be gathered into one place. We read in

Genesis 1:9-11, *"let dry ground appear." And it was so.* [10]*and God called the dry ground "land." Then God said, "Let the land produce vegetation."* The corollary implies that **there was now just one large land mass and one large ocean** region during this particular geological age that is referred to as the Third Day of Creation. This does not mean that during prior times that the continents were just one large supercontinent because the science of geology has confirmed that the Earth's crust has always been in a state of change right from its beginning to this point in time. See Figure 3-2.

The work necessary to culminate this plan is described at the closing of verse 9 & 12 as follows: "And it was so." This phrase is very significant, as it means that the work had now been completed by the Creator at the end of this Creation Day. The statement was not, for instance, that it may be so in the future, or was planned to be. Rather, "and it *was* so" means that the plan conceived by the Great Divine Architect was completed by the end of this Third Creation Day.

The finished work is then described in verse 10 as follows, *"And God called the dry land earth, and the gathering together of the waters He called seas. And God saw that it was good."* (Genesis 1:10, NIV)

The Geological Record Confirms the Bible Record

Genesis 1:9-13 describes three events, each of which is substantiated by the geological record of this age. **First**, dry land appeared. This implies, in geological terms, a regional rising of land areas to appear above sea level. **Second**, the waters of the Earth are described as being gathered together into one place, which **suggests the concept of one large ocean, and one large "super-continent."** This also provides the basis for the geological concept of continental drift / plate tectonics as we will see in later chapters. **Third**, land plants were created and formed. This can all be documented by the science of geology. It is believed that this particular age lasted about 120 million years. See Figure 1-1.

The First Land Plants

The work necessary to culminate the plan of Genesis 1:11 is likewise described as concluded for we read, "And it was so." Verse 12 then, describes the result of the work that was completed by repeating verse 11 almost word for word. The passage states that "the earth brought forth vegetation."

Verse 11 describes the creation of the first land plants on Earth. We read, *"Let the land produce vegetation: seed-bearing plants and trees on the land that bear fruit with seed in it, according to their various kinds. And it was so."* According to geology, there is no evidence of land plants on the Earth prior to the Upper Silurian, Devonian, Mississippian and the Pennsylvanian Periods. This all took place during the Third Creation Day. See Figures 1-1 and 3-2.

Geology verifies that there were two main types of land plants. They were the spore bearing and the seed bearing plants. It would appear as though the Creator created the fertile spores and seeds in the soil that brought forth the various species of land plants. They all reproduced offspring after their kind from generation to generation.

The King James translation and the New King James version mention the creation of grass and herbs, which is a misnomer. A more correct translation is provided in the New International Version as follows: *"The Land (earth) produced vegetation: plants bearing seed according to their kinds and trees bearing fruit with seed in it according to their kind. And God saw that it was good* (Genesis 1:12 NIV)

According to Walter Beasley[1], "*The Hebrew word translated as "grass" came from a root word which means "to sprout or to shoot." In later times, the word was used for ordinary grass, but, strictly speaking, any plant that shoots out of the earth could be described as "deshe" or "sproutage."*"[1] It is quite proper to say "Let the earth bring forth sproutage (or even vegetation)." Geology confirms that grasses and herbs did not appear on the Earth until Upper Cretaceous time, towards the latter part of the Fifth Day of Creation (see Figure 1-1).

When God observed His finished work of creation, He stated: *"And it was good."* (Genesis 1:12) Everything that God had created and made during the Third Day, as well as throughout the entire Six Days of Creation, had a significant, positive ecological influence and impact upon the Earth that was good.

The Bible is silent as to the technique God may have used to create living seeds and spores within the ground of the Earth. It is believed that He used the same method He used to create and form Man and Woman as well as all species of animal life. He formed (*Yatsar*) the body of the initial seed or spore out of previously existing material in the soil, and then created *(bara)* life within the seed or spore through the power of His spoken word.

A summation of the Third Day is given in the 13th verse of Genesis One:*[13] "And there was evening, and there was morning—the third day."* The evening refers to the time when God planned, or drew up an architectural blueprint, for this day. The morning relates to the time when God commenced the work necessary to bring this plan into fruition. It was during the day that all the work was completed. See APPENDIX C.

The Greenhouse Effect Continues

The greenhouse that was established on the Earth during the Second Day is believed to have continued throughout the Third Day. The dissipation of the greenhouse took place during the Fourth Creation Day when the establishment of the seasons took place.

Dunbar and Waage[2] describe the Earth's vegetation during this geological age as follows: *"One of the striking features of the Pennsylvanian flora was the marked similarity of the species in different parts of the world. They were nearly as cosmopolitan as any in the earth's history. It suggests the absence of well marked climate zones."* This information again lends credence to the presence of a "Greenhouse Effect" being firmly established at this time. Seasonal changes were yet to come.

The picture of the Earth that emerges during the Third Day is illustrated in Figure 3-1. The sun, moon and stars are present in the sky, but are not visible upon the face of the Earth. The sun is shining upon the heavy cloud cover on the Earth.

The blanket of clouds is believed to have caused warm, uniform temperature and warm climate conditions to prevail throughout the Earth. Sufficient rays from the sun were able to reach the Earth's surface to allow a healthy and luxuriant growth of land plants to flourish, and for photosynthesis to take place. Throughout the duration of the Third Day, there is no evidence of ice in any part of the Earth. In other words, God had established a "Greenhouse Effect" upon the entire Earth throughout this long period of time that is called the Third Creation Day.

The Regional Rising of the Land

The reference to a regional rising of the land is found in the second part of the 9th verse of Genesis 1 where God said: *"Let the waters under heaven be gathered together unto one place and let the dry land appear."*

There is clear evidence in the geological record for a regional rising of the land out of water on every continent during the Upper Silurian and the Early Devonian Period. This event is known as the Caledonian Orogeny in certain regions of the Earth. It was associated with mountain building activities in certain specific regions. For example, the Appalachian Mountains were beginning to form again at this time along the east coast of Canada and the United States, as was the Boothia Cornwallis Fold Belt in the Canadian Arctic Islands of Canada.

Throughout the Earth, there is generally a pronounced break, or erosion surface, which separates the underlying Lower & Middle Silurian sediments from the overlying Devonian sediments. This erosion surface is so pronounced and extensive that the Silurian and Ordovician rocks have been partially removed. In some areas these sediments have been completely removed by erosion before the overlying Devonian sediments were deposited.

There are local deep basin areas where continual deposition did take place throughout this period, but they are very rare. For example, the well known Royal Creek Section in the Northern Yukon Territory of Northern Canada was an area of continuous deposition. Paleontologists from many parts of the world desire to see this Royal Creek Section of Upper Silurian Age to discover the forms of life that were present during this particular age. I had the privilege of being on a Geological Field Party in the northern Yukon Territories just to the north of the Royal Creek Section. However, I was never at the site. This site is located to the south of the north-south trending Richardson Mountains in the Bonnet Plume Basin. See Figure 3-4.

Continental Drift / Plate Tectonics

The concept of continental drift was first advocated by certain persons in the early part of this century. It attempted to explain the movement of Earth's continents relative to each other. The Google website says, "*The hypothesis that continents 'drift' was first put forward by* Abraham Ortelius *in 1596 and was fully developed by* Alfred Wegener *in 1912. However, it was not until the development of the theory of* plate tectonics *in the 1960s, that a sufficient* geological *explanation of that movement was found.*"

Google says, "*It is now known that there are two kinds of crust,* continental crust *and* oceanic crust. *Continental crust is inherently lighter and of a different composition to oceanic crust, but both kinds reside above a much deeper fluid mantle. Oceanic crust is created at* spreading centers, *and this, along with* subduction, *drives the system of plates in a chaotic manner, resulting in continuous* orogeny *and areas of isostatic imbalance. The theory of* plate tectonics *explains all this, including the movement of the continents, better than Wegener's theory.*"

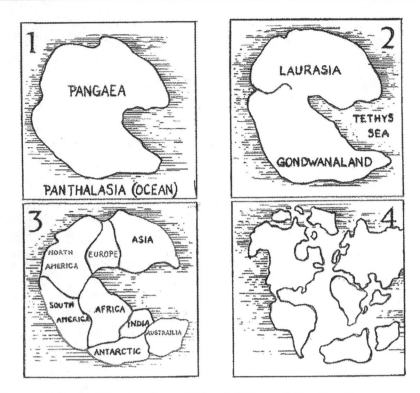

Figure 3-2: An Illustration of the drifting of the Continents, now called "Plate Tectonics."

Window No. 1: reveals Archean to end of Middle Silurian plate tectonics.

Window No. 2: reveals Upper Silurian to end of Pennsylvanian plate tectonics.

Window No. 3: reveals the Permian plate tectonics.

Window No. 4: reveals Triassic, Jurassic & Cretaceous plate tectonics. Separation continued into the Cenozoic.

First scenario is No.1: During the Archean, Proterozoic, Cambrian, Ordovician and the Lower and Middle Silurian ages geologists relate the then existing super continental region of the Earth to a place called Pangaea. The surrounding low lying region of the Earth was called Panthalasia. Once ocean water appeared on Earth at the beginning of the Proterozoic

Age, then Panthalasia became known as the ocean region and Pangaea as the land region. This early geological age scenario also relates directly to the First and Second Days of Creation. See Figures 3-2 & 1-1.

Second Scenario is No. 2: During the Upper Silurian, Devonian, Mississippian and Pennsylvanian Periods of time, the Tethys Sea began to encroach from the east causing Pangaea to divide into a northern region called Laurasia and a southern region called Gondwanaland. This age relates directly to the Third Creation Day.

Third Scenario is No. 3: During the Permian Period major breakages or rift valleys began to take place. North and South America began to break away or to rift from Europe and Africa. India and Antarctica began to rift away from Africa. Also Australia began to rift away from India and Antarctica. Geology verifies that these major rift valleys were in filled with great volumes of sediments in the order of 8000+feet (2438+meters) in thickness. However, during the Permian Age the complete separation of the continents was not yet evident. This geologic age relates directly with the Fourth Creation Day.

Fourth Scenario is No. 4: During the Triassic, Jurassic, Cretaceous, Tertiary and Quaternary Periods the continued rifting has resulted in complete and a continuing separation of the continents as shown on Figure 3-2. This time period relates directly to the Fifth and Sixth Creation Days. This entire process is referred to as plate tectonics. I would advise the reader to go to Google for more specific information.

Characteristic Geological Formations

Sedimentary rocks of the Upper Silurian have been eroded or were never deposited in most parts of the Earth except for local areas. This was due to a regional rising of the land regions. See Figure 3-3. The overlying sediments of the

Devonian, Mississippian and Pennsylvanian Periods range in thickness from a few thousand feet to more than 25,000 feet (7,620m) in local regions within the North American continent. About 8%, of the world's oil and 25% of the world's gas has been found in rocks of the Devonian and Mississippian ages. Much of the conventional oil in Western Canada is produced from rocks of this age.

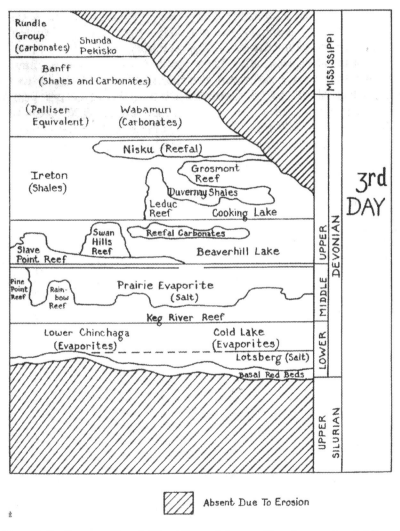

Figure 3-3: Generalized Stratigraphic section in central Alberta, Canada, showing some of the rock units & formations represented by the 3rd Creation Day. Prepared by Don Daae.

The total thickness of the Devonian sediments in Western Canada ranges between 2500 to 4000 feet (762-1219m). A portion of the Devonian section is shown on Figure 3-3.

The famous Leduc Reef in the Province of Alberta, Canada is a prolific oil and gas reservoir. The Leduc pinnacle reefs are about 1000+ feet (304.8+ meters) in height from top to bottom, consisting of limestone with abundant reef building organisms. It is an outgrowth of the underlying Cooking Lake Formation, which is also a reef forming limestone about 150 to 300 feet (46-92m) in thickness. These reefs as well as the adjacent Grosmont reef are surrounded by the shales of the Ireton and the Duvernay Formations that form an excellent seal for oil.

The Beaverhill Lake Formation is about 700 feet (213m) thick underlying the Cooking Lake Formation. It is a shale unit, except for two reef units, referred to as the Slave Point and the Swan Hills Reefs, both of which produce oil and gas in Alberta. See Figure 3-3.

Underlying the Beaverhill Lake is the Prairie Evaporate (salt/ potash) unit, about 400 to 500 feet (122-152m) in thickness, which in turn is underlain by the Winnipegosis / Keg River Reefs. This latter reef unit is very vuggy and produces oil in northwestern Alberta and northeast British Columbia. Below are the salt and anhydrite beds of the Cold Lake / Chinchaga / Lotsburg, and the Basal Red Bed Formations.

These geological formations of Devonian age were deposited under normal conditions in a marine environment very similar to reefs that are being developed in the Caribbean and other areas of the Earth today. The period of time involved in their formation is very significant.

Earth scientists, who have studied modern reefs, have found that under optimum conditions, the most rapid reef growth is about 3 to 5 centimeters (1.2 to 2 inches) per year. Under these conditions, it would take as long as 10,000 Years to deposit a reef 1000 feet thick. This, of course, does not include or allow the time when erosion or non deposition was occurring on the reef front.

The First Land Plants

At the same time as God instructed the dry land to appear, He also created and formed the first land plants. In Genesis 1:11 (NKJV), God said, "*Let the earth bring forth sproutage, the herb yielding seed, and the fruit tree yielding fruit after his kind, whose seed is in itself, upon the earth and it was so.*"

The first occurrence of land plants in the geological record is found in association with the rising of the land during the Upper Silurian Age. See Figure 3-4. These plants are distinguished from marine plants in that they had vascular bundles to transport fluids from the roots throughout its upper members. According to Gray and Boucot:[3] "*Within the Silurian, the few megafossils attributed to vascular plants commonly lack definite criteria such as cutinized spores, tracheids, and epidermal cuticle with stomates; such remains are known only from Late Silurian occurrences in Britain, Czechoslovakia, Podolia and New York.*"

Plant spores have been found in the Lower Silurian, as well as the Upper Ordovician, in Bohemia, which are similar to the spores in plants that have vascular bundles, but there is a lack of supporting evidence in the actual vegetative and other remains. These spores could have belonged to certain marine algae, especially the red algae (Rhodephyte). Gray and Boucot[4] say, "*Truly non-marine Early Silurian environments have not yet yielded spores. It remains for future work to determine whether or not plant spores will be recovered in sufficient abundance from non-marine early Silurian beds to warrant the conclusion that plants had already invaded the land.*"

THE BIBLICAL RECORD	THE GEOLOGICAL RECORD			INTERPRETATION
	PERIOD	EVIDENCE	STRATIGRAPHY	
The 4th Day	280 Myr		Marine Shoreline Continental deposits	
The 3rd Day — "Let the earth bring forth sproutage." Gen. 1:11 — "Let all the waters be gathered together in one place." Gen.1:9 — "Let the dry land appear." Gen. 1:9	Penn-sylv-anian U M L; Miss-issipp-ian U L; Devon-ian U M L; Silurian U 400 Myr	One super ocean & one continent — Support of Greenhouse — Ferns, scale trees, cordaites, scouring rushes	Crinoidal Limestone; Reefs; nondeposition or erosion; Sigillaria, Lepido-, Cordaites, dendron, Horse Tails, Stegocephalian, Ferns; 1ST LAND PLANTS	There were many separate acts of Special Creation of plant and animal life throughout the 3rd Day
The 2nd Day	Silur-ian M L		CALEDONIAN OROGENY	

Figure 3-4: Plant & Animal Life created during the 3rd Day of Creation. According to Dunbar and Waage,[5] "From the coal measures of North America alone, no fewer than 7 orders, 19 families, 46 genera, and 88 species are known." Prepared by Don Daae.

For clarification of the geological time periods cited in these extracts, please refer to Figure 1-1.

Before Devonian times, the evidence of land plants is very meager, and concerns only small herbaceous types of plants called psilopsids. Definite species of land plants have not been found in rocks prior to the Upper Silurian time.

From the early Devonian and onward, the record of land plants is clear and abundant. Psilopsids were present during the Lower Devonian. They were small, leafless, spore bearing land plants about a foot or so in height, with vascular bundles and no developed root system. Photosynthesis took place in the stem, and horizontal portions of the stem ran along the ground to serve the function of roots. A modern psilopsid is found living today in the tropic regions.

By the Middle Devonian, a considerable diversity of trees had spread over the land areas of the Earth. Spore-bearing varieties of ferns, scale trees, and some scouring rushes have been identified. True ferns have been found in Middle Devonian sandstones on the north slope of the Catskill Mountains in the State of New York where a significant number of tree stumps, some more than 30 feet (9 m) high and more than 2 feet (60 cm) in diameter at the base were found still standing where they grew. This undoubtedly indicates rapid burial, probably related to sudden and more local flood conditions.

By Pennsylvanian time, lush vegetation spread over the moist lowland areas of the Earth. See Figure 1-1. The giants of the time were strange, spore-bearing trees (like the ferns), the scouring rushes, and the scale trees.

Coal beds of this age are found in northern Europe and England, as well as in the State of Pennsylvania in the United States. The coal is known as anthracite, often referred to as "hard coal." Less indurated coal, like bituminous, is found in rocks of the Mesozoic Era. Whereas, in the younger Tertiary beds, a soft coal called lignite is found. Generally speaking, the older the geological formation, the harder and more indurated is the quality of the coal.

Scale Trees

The scale trees were the most impressive and the most common plants during the Third Day. They were up to 100 feet (30.5m) in height, with trunks up to 6 feet (2 m) in diameter at the base. Most of these scale trees belonged to either the lepidodendron or sigillaria varieties and they were all greatly reduced in importance during the colder weather of the Lower Permian. They then became extinct by the end of the Permian Age. This equates to the end of the Fourth Day. See Figure 1-1. See Dunbar & Waage[6] for greater details.

The lepidodendron trees grew a small, slender trunk, branching repeatedly near the top to present a spreading crown of stubby twigs covered with slender, strap-like leaves. The leaves were 6 to 8 inches (15-20 cm) long and about one-half inch (1 cm) wide. The shed leaves left sharply defined diamond-shaped leaf scars which were arranged in spiral rows about the limbs and trunk. Spore cases were borne as cones at the tips of the limbs. When these tree trunks were first found, it was thought they were fossilized snake skins.

The sigillaria tree possessed a thicker trunk which rarely branched. It was clothed for several feet from the top with large, blade-like leaves, resembling those of the lepidodendron, but larger. The bark was vertically ribbed, and the leaf scars were normally in vertical rows. Trunks have been found up to 6 feet (2 m) in diameter at the base, and up to 100 feet (30.5m) long without a branch.

Scouring Rushes

The largest of the scouring rushes was the variety known as calamites. Some attained a height of 30 feet (9 m) and 12 inches (30 cm) in diameter. Their trunks were not solid, woody stems, but rather thin, woody cylinders filled with a core of pith and surrounded by thick bark. The woody layer was sometimes up to 2 inches (5 cm) thick. Smaller varieties of the scouring rushes were called "horsetails," some of which have persisted to the present day (Figure 1-1).

Ferns

There were many varieties of ferns beginning in Early Devonian and becoming more numerous throughout the Mississippian and Pennsylvanian Periods, giving a lush cover to the land. Some ferns grew to be as high as 50 feet

(15.2m), with fronds reaching a length of 6 feet (1.82 m) (see Figure 1-1).

The seed ferns resembled the true spore bearing ferns in every respect, except that they bore small, nut-like seeds instead of spores. Seed ferns first appeared during the Mississippian and were more common than the spore-bearing ferns during the Pennsylvanian. They became scarce after the Permian and became extinct during the Triassic Age.

The spore bearing ferns (pteropsids) first appeared during the Devonian. They are often referred to as the true ferns. However, the fact that they were spore bearing differentiates them from the seed ferns. They reproduced by means of spores that are shed from spore cases on the undersides of the leaves. These ferns were among the most common of the Devonian plants. Some varieties grew to 40 feet (12.2m) in height and were tree-like, whereas other varieties were small. These ferns constituted much of the underbrush of the coal swamps during the Pennsylvanian age. Of the spore-bearing plants of the Third Day, they are the only group to persist in abundance to the present day. See Dunbar & Waage[7] for greater details.

Cordaite Trees

The cordaite trees were tall and graceful, with some attaining a height of 120 feet (36.6m) and a diameter of 3 feet (1.0 m). They are similar to the modern conifer, except for two main respects. Firstly, their leaves were not needle-like, but blade-like, attaining a length of several inches to 6 feet (2m). Secondly, their seeds were formed in racemes instead of being crowded into cones. The wood of the cordaite trees were much like that of modern pine, but the pith at the centre was larger. They were the main contributor to the vegetation which made the Pennsylvanian coal, and became extinct by the end of the Permian Age. (see Figure 1-1). See Dunbar & Waage[8] for greater detail.

Conifers

The first true conifer or evergreen trees appeared during the Pennsylvanian Period, but are found in only a few localities. It has been suggested that they may have lived in the uplands rather than the swampy lowlands, and were, therefore, not commonly preserved.

Coal Beds

During the Pennsylvanian period, great beds of coal were deposited on a worldwide basis. Dunbar and Waage[9] say, *"It was no accident that in both Europe and North America the Pennsylvanian rocks are known as the coal measures. No other geologic system contains so much high rank coal. In these formations lie the great coal fields of the British Isles, of the Saar Basin in France, of the Ruhr Basin of Germany and Belgium, and of the Donetz Basin in Russia. In North America it includes the vast coalfields of Oklahoma and Kansas to the Appalachian Mountains. These fields in Europe and America produce more than 80% of the world's coal."* The thickness of the sediments of the Third Day and the thickness of the Pennsylvanian coal beds are mind boggling. Truly, this was a time of lush vegetation throughout the Earth.

First True Vertebrates

The Bible is silent about other major events at this time, such as the appearance of vertebrate fish, amphibians, early reptiles and insects. However, where the Bible is silent, the Earth speaks. The science of geology, paleontology, palynology and associated sciences are able to describe and to discover new information. It is truly amazing how all of this information compliments and gives added insights into the accuracy of the Bible record.

There are three classes of vertebrates that appeared during the Third Day: **the placoderms, the sharks, and the bony fish**. The sharks and the bony fish were true vertebrates in that they all had a vertebral column with a notochord. They, thus, can be identified with the Chordate Phyla that originated during the Lower Cambrian Explosion of Animal Life.

Placoderms: Placoderms first appeared in the Upper Silurian rocks, and are the first jaw-bearing fish. They had a tough, bony external armor whose exact function is unknown. They had a partially calcified vertebrae and internal bones that are often fossilized. Most species were small; from one to a few feet in length, however, one giant species reached a length of 30 feet (9.1m) and had a mouth several feet wide. They reached their peak of abundance and variety in the Middle Devonian and began to decline rapidly in Late Devonian and became extinct during the Permian.

Sharks: Sharks first appeared during the Devonian Period. They were true vertebrates. However, their vertebrae and internal bones were made entirely of tough, calcified, organic cartilage. Thus, they have a fairly poor fossil record. However, some teeth and external spines have been found. Their calcified remains are common in certain marine sedimentary rock. They have continued to survive to the present.

Golden Age of Fish: Bony Fish first appeared during the Devonian Age. The Devonian is often considered the "Golden Age of Fish." They were true vertebrates in that they had a spinal column with a notochord. They are differentiated into two groups: the "ray finned" and "lobe finned." The ray finned bony fish includes almost all the present day bony fish. Many of these species have continued to the present. The lobe finned fish were abundant during Devonian time and then declined thereafter.

All of the above marine species appeared suddenly in the fossil record, fully specialized, with a complete absence of transitional forms. Thus, the fossil record strongly supports the concept that they were indeed created by the Great Divine Creator of the universe.

The First Land Animals

First Amphibians: Labyrinthodont Amphibians were the first true vertebrate animals that were at home in the water and also on land. They appeared suddenly during the Upper Devonian Period. They were most numerous during the Carboniferous Age when they became the dominant land vertebrates. The labyrinthodonts were present from the Upper Devonian to the end of the Triassic Period when they mysteriously became extinct. See Figure 1-1.

Abundant skeletal remains of small amphibians (resembling modern salamanders) are also present in rocks of the Pennsylvanian Age. Nearly all these amphibians are small only a few inches (cms) in length. The small amphibians were unlike modern day salamanders in that they had a cuirass of bony plates over the skull and had Labyrinthodont teeth.

There were also some larger amphibians about the size of a Florida alligator. They attained a length of 10 feet (3.0 m).

The common modern amphibians, such as frogs, toads, newts and salamanders originated much later during the Triassic and Jurassic ages that relate to the Fifth Creation Day. See Figure 1-1.

First Reptiles: The first reptiles appear in strata of Early Pennsylvanian age. One variety is called cotylosaur. They were small and lizard-like in appearance with a dentition indicative of a carnivorous animal. A second variety was the pelycosaur synapsids. They became the dominant reptiles of the Late Pennsylvanian and Early Permian Periods. Two species of pelycosaurs have been identified. One was called dimetrodon. It was a carnivore. The second was called edaphosaurus. It was an herbivore. They both had long, neural spines on their vertebrae which apparently supported a web of skin. These two reptiles have been given the popular name of "finbacks," and were the first reptiles to have canine teeth.

All of the above mentioned marine and land vertebrate species appeared suddenly in the fossil record, fully specialized, with a complete absence of transitional forms. Thus, the fossil record strongly supports the concept that they were indeed created by the Great Divine Creator of the universe.

First Insects

The first insects are recorded during this age. They were particularly abundant during the Pennsylvanian Age. About 400 species of insects have been recovered from the swamp sediments associated with the thick coal measures. Cockroaches were the most common insects. One species was about four inches in length. Dragonflies were common and exceptionally large. One species had a wingspan of 29 inches (73cm). As a whole, insects have not been as large during any other age. Scorpions, spiders, and centipedes have also been found in these sedimentary rocks.

In Conclusion

The Bible record of the Third Day of Creation directs our attention to three major significant events: the worldwide rising of the land, the worldwide gathering together of the waters into one super ocean, the creation of the first land plants and the creation of new species of animal life. All these events are confirmed and supported by the geological record. They provide a framework into which it is possible to relate them to a specific geological age of the Earth and likewise to the Bible record. (Figure 1-1)

The Bible is silent as to the creation of great numbers of animal species such as fish, amphibians, early reptiles and large numbers of insects and invertebrate life during the Third Day. However, the psalmist states *"Truth shall spring out of the earth and righteousness shall look down from heaven"* (Psalm 85:11 NKJV). This "truth," or "faithfulness," means that the Earth is faithful in recording the great numbers of new species of plant and animal life micro and macro that were designed, created, formed and made by the Master Creator of the Universe according to the plan set out by the Amazing Architect.

Plant and animal life are transitory, living for a brief period of time, and becoming a part of the geological record as fossils. Through a thorough examination of rocks, an earth scientist is able to reconstruct what these vast numbers of plant and animal species were like, providing details which are beyond the scope of the Bible and beyond the scope of this book to describe.

The fossil record reveals that the hundreds of new species of plant and animal life were not created at one moment in time as Creation Science people maintain. They appear suddenly, fully developed, and highly specialized at many different time intervals throughout the Third Day. Each new species of animal life (micro and macro) are able to fit into one of the 35 or so phyla or body plans that were established and have now been identified with the Cambrian Explosion of Animal Life that took place during the Lower Cambrian Age. See Figures 1-1 and 1-4.

References for the Third Day

1. Beasley Walter, F.R.G.S., "AMAZING ARCHITECT," Marshall, Morgan, & Scott, Ltd., London & Edinburgh, 1955, p.28.
2. Dunbar Carl O. and Waage Karl M., *Historical Geology*, Third Edition (New York: John Wiley and Sons, Inc., 1969), Dunbar and Waage, p. 281.
3. Jane Gray and A.T, Boucot, "Early Silurian Spore Tetrads from New York: Earliest New World Evidence for Vascular Plants," Science, Vol. 173, Sept. 1971, p. 919,
4. Gray and Boucot, p. 921.
5. Dunbar & Waage. p. 283.
6. Dunbar & Waage, pp. 279-281.
7. Dunbar & Waage, p. 276.
8. Dunbar & Waage, p. 281.
9. Dunbar & Waage, p. 269-270.

Chapter 4

The Fourth Day of Creation

Introduction

The Fourth Day represents a time of great changes in climate throughout the Earth. It marks the end of the warm and moist climate encouraged by the "Green House Effect" that prevailed throughout most of the Second and Third Creation Days. Seasons were established upon the Earth during the Fourth Day. This is a fact verified by the geological record. As a whole, the Fourth Day corresponds to the geological Permian Period. See Figures 1-1 and 4-1.

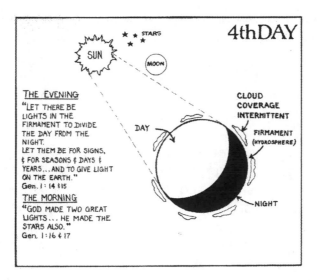

Figure 4-1: An illustration of the Biblical 4th Day of Creation

The Bible Record

God made three things happen during this time. First, he made the sun to rule the day; second, he made the moon to rule the night; and third, he made the stars.

There may appear to be a contradiction here. We have learned before that God created the sun, moon and stars during the First Day. Thus, it is important that we examine the Biblical record of this day in Genesis One to see what actually took place. We read in Genesis 1:14-19, "*14And God said, Let there be lights in the firmament of heaven to divide the day from the night; and let them be for signs, and for seasons, and for days and years: 15And let them be for lights in the firmament of the heaven to give light upon the earth: and it was so. 16And God made two great lights; the greater light to rule the day, and the lesser light to rule the night; he made the stars also. 17And God set them in the firmament of the heaven to give light upon the earth. 18And to rule over the day and over the night, and to divide the light from the darkness: and God saw that it was good. 19And the evening and the morning were the fourth day.*"

The Bible is directing our attention toward worldwide changes in climate and the establishment of seasons as we know them today. It is interesting to note that God did not create (*bara*) the sun, moon and stars, but he made (*asah*) the sun, moon and stars during the Fourth Day of Creation. What is the difference? See Figure 1-15.

The Hebrew word that denotes absolute origination is *bara*. It means to create something out of no previous existing materials. Bara is not used during the Fourth Day; the word *asah* (made) is used instead.

Asah gives a clue as to what is taking place. The use of this word supposes that the sun, moon and stars were already in existence. They had already experienced a prior creation (*bara*) and secondly that they had gone through the processes of *yatsar*, of being formed and molded. *Asah* has great latitude in that it means to do, to make, to accomplish, to advance, to appoint, bring forth, etc. Campbell G. Morgan[1] says, "*Asah also refers to things which are manipulated into new forms.*"

The definition that best applies to this day is the word appoint. God gave the sun, moon and stars a new appointment, or a new assignment. They were created during the First Creation Day, but now something new was in the process of taking place. God was now beginning to disperse the cloud coverage and was now allowing the sun, moon and stars to shine through the firmament of heaven (hydrosphere) to give light directly upon the Earth, and to rule over the day and over the night. The picture that is portrayed is illustrated in Figure 4-1.

The blanket of clouds that surrounded the Earth during the Second and Third Days or more specifically from the Upper Silurian to the end of the Carboniferous Age was now terminated. This resulted in the release of great amounts of water. In this process, the heavy cloud coverage began to disperse allowing the sun, moon and stars to shine directly upon the face of the Earth once again. It is also postulated here, that the release of water resulted in a cooling of the atmosphere that in turn precipitated the great Permian Ice Age.

With the disbursement of the clouds, the sun, moon and stars were able to shine directly upon the surface of the Earth, which had been obscured during the Second and Third Days by cloud cover. The Bible record states "*God set them in the firmament of the heaven TO GIVE LIGHT UPON THE EARTH*" (Genesis 1:17 NKJV). The firmament refers to the hydrosphere, which is that portion of the atmosphere that is able to sustain plant and animal life. From the vantage point of standing on the Earth, the sun, moon, and stars would have appeared to be set in the firmament. These lights were assigned certain "responsibilities." They were to divide the day from the night, and were to determine periods of time and events, such as YEARS, DAYS, SEASONS and SIGNS (Genesis 1:14).

The length of a year, day, or season is determined by the relationship between the motions of the Earth, sun, moon and stars. A year is the time it takes for the Earth to make one complete orbit around the sun. The length of a day is determined by the time it takes for the Earth to make one complete rotation on its axis; and thus we have day and night, morning and evening. The concept of a month is lunar in origin.

The Bible says in Psalm 104:19 (NKJV) that "*He appointed the moon for seasons*". According to our present calendar, there are 12 lunar months during a year, which provides a basis for marking the passage of the seasons; summer, winter, fall and spring. Calendar keeping has changed dramatically over the centuries, but the general principles of reckoning based on the motions of the Earth and moon in relation to the sun, have remained the same.

The stars are sometimes used by God for "signs." When Christ was born in Bethlehem, the star was a sign to the Wise Men from the east that a Saviour and King had been born.

Christ said that prior to his second coming there will be "*signs in the sun, and in the moon, and in the stars, and upon the earth distress of nations with perplexities, the sea and the waves roaring. Men's hearts failing them for fear and for looking after those things which are coming on the earth, for the powers of heaven shall be shaken, and then shall they see the Son of Man coming in a cloud with power and great Glory*" (Luke 21:25-27). Thus, Christ is confirming that the sun, moon and stars are sometimes used by God for signs.

Astronomers sometime refer to the signs of the Zodiac. These are the different constellations, or groups of stars, that lie along the ecliptic. Now, the term ecliptic refers to the path of the Earth as it travels through space over the course of one year.

The twelve signs of the Zodiac are traversed as the Earth travels in its orbit around the sun, thus the seasons can be known by whatever sign of the Zodiac is at the zenith. The Bible refers to the signs of the Zodiac by the name of Mazzaroth: *"Canst thou bring forth Mazzaroth IN HIS SEASON."* (Job 38:32) The Bible does not attach any religious significance to the signs of the Zodiac other than for determining seasons.

The Geological Record

The Permian Period was a time of dramatic change throughout the world. This geological age lasted about 55 million years based upon radioactive methods of dating. This age brought the entire Paleozoic Era to a dramatic close. See Figure 1-1.

Geology confirms the establishment of worldwide seasonal changes during the early part of the Permian Period which relates to the Fourth Creation Day. See Figure 1-1. This is based on a few key observations. First, the trees from the Permian Age to the present day reveal well established seasonal tree rings, whereas the trees prior to this time from the Devonian and Carboniferous Periods lack seasonal rings.

Some of the trees that lived during the previous Carboniferous Age were over 120 feet (49m) high and had tree trunks up to 6 feet (2m) in diameter, **but lacked seasonal rings** as we know them today. Several authors have made mention of the **establishment of tree rings** beginning in the Early Mesozoic and the lack of seasonal rings in the Paleozoic trees. Walter Beasley[2] says, *"From the Mesozoic Era, the geologists find seasons permanently established and new types of trees becoming features in it. The seasonal rings, which became permanent features in the new vegetation, and the arrival of altogether new types of living things, bear testimony to the tremendous climatic changes noted at this time for which no satisfactory scientific explanation has been given."*[2]

NO SEASONAL RINGS ARE PRESENT IN FOSSIL TREES OF PENNSYLVANIAN OR OLDER AGE

SEASONAL TREE RINGS ARE WELL ESTABLISHED IN THE MESOZOIC

Figure 4-2: The establishment of seasons during the 4th Day is confirmed by the well developed seasonal rings of the Permian & Mesozoic Periods and the absence of tree rings in the former Pennsylvanian and older ages.

Dunbar and Waage[3] describe the Carboniferous vegetation as follows, *"The trees, whether tree ferns, seed ferns, chordates, or the great scale trees, bore succulent foliage* *of almost unprecedented luxuriance. Not merely were the leaves large, but their texture indicates rapid growth under warm, humid conditions. For example, the very large size of the individual cells, the arrangement of the stomata (breathing pores), the smoothness and thickness of the bark, the presence of aerial roots, **AND THE ABSENCE OF GROWTH RINGS** in the woody trunks are all features of significance."*[3]

The Great Permian Ice Age

During the Lower Permian, which corresponds to the early part of the Fourth Creation Day (Figure 1-1), large portions of the Southern Hemisphere became covered by a giant sheet of glacial ice several thousands of feet (meters) thick. See Figure 4-3.

Geology also confirms that this ice age also extended into the Middle Permian age. Dunbar & Waage[4] say, "*Large portions of the southern hemisphere throughout Gondwanaland were covered with a thick sheet of ice up to several thousands of feet thick.*" To be more specific, major portions of Antarctica, most of Australia, a greater part of India, the southeast portion of South America, the southern third of Africa and Madagascar were covered by ice at this time.

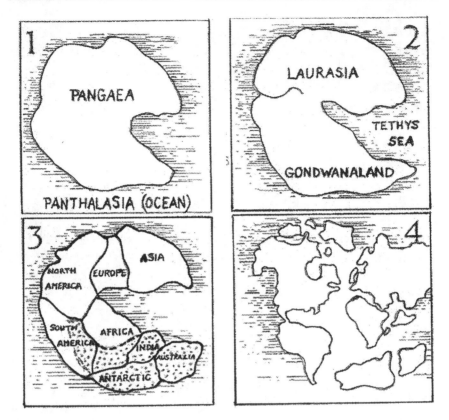

Figure 4-3: During the Lower Permian, Glacial Ice covered Gondwanaland which included Antarctica, Australia, India, Southern Africa and portions of South America as shown in window 3 above.

By the latter part of the Middle Permian, the climate had warmed sufficiently to melt the ice and to bring this great ice age to a close. Evidence of ice in the Northern Hemisphere at this time has not been found, but it is believed that the North Pole would have been centered in the ocean area, whereas Gondwanaland was centered in the southern polar region. The land areas to the north on Figure 4-3 would have escaped Glaciation.

During the Permian Age, the continents to the north of the glacial ice consisted of intermittent, large, dry desert plains occupied by shifting sand dunes and delta fans formed by seasonal torrents. Temporary lakes and evaporitic salt pools were present. Great thicknesses of salt are found locally in rocks of Permian age.

The prevailing red color of the sandstones and clays of the Middle and Upper Permian indicate that warm and dry conditions prevailed on most lands. Even the areas that were covered by ice during the Lower and Middle Permian were now experiencing warm and often dry conditions. For example, Dunbar and Waage[5] report that "*In South Africa—the Upper Permian has a great variety of reptiles that indicate an appreciably warmer climate.*" This same area experienced Glaciation during the Lower and Middle Permian.

It is important to note that there were certain parts of the Earth experiencing temperate and tropical climate conditions with abundant precipitation. Also, reef growth was active in certain local areas. As a general rule the climate was radically changed from that which prevailed during the Third Day from the base of the Ordovician to the end of the Pennsylvanian Period. See Figure 1-1.

Earth's Crust Experienced Severe Trauma

During Permian time, the Earth's crust experienced severe trauma in many places. Dunbar and Waage[6] say, "*Momentous changes ushered the Paleozoic to a close. As the mobile borderlands continued to rise; several of the great Paleozoic geosynclines were uplifted and transformed into ranges of folded mountains. While the Appalachians were forming in eastern America, the Urals were rising out of a great geosyncline in Eastern Europe and other ranges were growing across southern Europe and southern Asia. By the close of Permian time all the continents were completely emergent, deserts were widespread and the world had experienced the most severe and widespread glaciation of Phanerozoic time . . . . Judged by the changes that occurred, the end of the Paleozoic Era was one of the great crises in the history of the earth."* Then Dunbar & Waage[7] say, *"West Texas and eastern New Mexico were occupied by a rapidly subsiding basin in which Permian deposits accumulated to a thickness of about 14,000 feet (4,267.2m), of which all but the uppermost division is marine,"*

Plant Life

Something happened at the beginning of the Fourth Day which caused many species of land plants to come to a relatively sudden end. The large scale trees (lepidodendron and sigillaria) as well as the cordaite trees of the Carboniferous (Third Day) became extinct. Their place was taken by other plants which gave a new face to the plant world. Beasley quotes J.W. Howchin[8] who says, *"Physical changes took place over much of the earth's surface towards the close of the Carboniferous Period and extended over most of the Permo-Carboniferous Period, which created a crisis in the vegetable world. Something happened by which this cosmopolitan flora came to a relatively sudden end and its place was taken by other plants which gave a new facies to the vegetable world. What led to such a sweeping change in plant life at that time is not definitely known, but there is a high probability that it was caused by important modifications in the physical conditions of the earth's surface, especially in relation to climate.*[8]

Animal Life

Insects: There were many new insects that were generally smaller than those in the previous age. Dunbar & Waage[9] say, *"No less than 20 orders have been described from Insect hill near Elmo, Kansas and most of these are also present in the USSR and Australia . . . . One of the dragonflies had a wingspread of 13 inches (32 cm)."* These many new species were designed, formed and created by the Great Divine Architect and Creator of the universe.

Amphibians: A Lower Permian Labyrinthodont (amphibian) from Texas was about 5 feet (1.52 cm) long. There were other smaller varieties or species of amphibians, but they all had broad heads and were of a different species from the Carboniferous amphibians of the Third Day. They all had a vertebral column and were true vertebrates.

Reptiles: Dunbar & Waage[10] say, "*Most of the Permian reptiles had long bodies, long tails and short legs.—The most bizarre were the pelycosaurs or finbacks.*" It was not until the Middle Permian that the Therapsid reptiles appeared. They flourished through Late Permian times, especially in the southern hemisphere. Their skeletal structure was generally reptilian, but they possessed some morphological features of primitive mammals and therefore are often referred to as mammal-like reptiles. Instead of walking with their elbows and knees stuck out in the sprawling, inefficient gait of other reptiles, they were able to move with their legs directly under their bodies. It is believed by some that most therapsid reptiles were small, agile carnivores. Dunbar & Waage[11] say, "*The Therapsid reptiles are known chiefly from the Upper Permian sediments in South Africa and from the Permian Basin in the U.S.S.R.*"

Invertebrates: The marine invertebrates from the preceding age continued to flourish throughout the Permian Period. There were also many new species of invertebrates that suddenly appeared. As a result of these new species of invertebrate life, Paleontologists are able to distinguish sediments of older and younger sediments by the fossil content.

Major Extinctions of Animal Life

Great changes took place in the animal world which caused multiple extinctions of Paleozoic life. Clark and Stearn[12] say, "*At the end of the Paleozoic Era many types of marine invertebrates died out, but other groups continued unchanged into the Mesozoic Era. N.D. Newell has said that "the wholesale extinction of major groups at the close of the Permian period in some ways marks the most critical time in invertebrate history since the early Cambrian. The cause of these extinctions is one of the major problems of paleontology."*[12]

Another authority N. M. Newall[13] writes as follows, *"One of the great groups of animals that disappeared at this time was the fusulinids, complex protozoans that ranged from microscopic sizes to 2-3 inches (5-8 cm) in length. They had populated the shallow seas of the world for 80 million years; their shells, piling up on the ocean floor, had formed vast deposits of limestone. The spiny brachiopods, likewise plentiful in the Late Paleozoic seas, also vanished without descendants. These and many other groups dropped suddenly from a state of dominance to one of oblivion. By the close of the Permian, 75 percent of the amphibian families and more than 80 percent of the reptile families had also disappeared."*[13]

THE BIBLICAL RECORD		THE GEOLOGICAL RECORD			INTERPRETATION
		PERIOD	EVIDENCE	STRATIGRAPHY	
The 5th Day		Triassic 225 m.yrs		Marine Shoreline Continental deposits	
The 4th Day	*"Let them be for signs, seasons, days and years"* Gen. 1:14 *"God made the (sun, moon & stars)— He set them in the firmament to give light upon the Earth."* Gen.1:16,17	P E R M I A N U _ L 280 m.yrs	Seasons Established Warm, arid conditions locally moist A major ice Age (cool) Worldwide changes in climate	Mass Extinction of Paleozoic Life salt & anhydrite reptiles conifers amphibians glacial till cordaites ferns	There were many separate acts of Special Creation of plant and animal life throughout the 4th Day
The 3rd Day		Pennsyl- vanian			

Figure 4-4: The sediments of the 4th Day are up to 8,000+ feet (2,438+m) in thickness along the east/west trending Dave Lord Ridge Permian rift basin in the Northern Yukon Territories of Canada. There were mass extinctions of animal life at the termination of the Permian Age. Prepared by Don Daae.

Speaking of these changes, Dunbar and Waage[14] state the following: *"The mass extinctions of major groups of animals, both on the land and in the sea, marks the close of the Paleozoic Era as one of the great crises in the history of life, and the reason is still an enigma. Drastic changes in the environment, both physical and climatic, might seem to be a probable reason were it not for the fact that the Glaciation was over near the beginning of Middle Permian time and the great expansion of the reptiles occurred later. Moreover, the marine invertebrates had made remarkable specializations adapting to the changing environment all through the period."*

Earth scientists are able to describe the great changes that took place during the Permian Period, but as yet have not found a satisfactory explanation as to why these changes took place.

The Cambrian Explosion Impact

Geology confirms that many new species of invertebrate life came into being during the Fourth Day of Creation. New species of amphibians and reptiles appeared at different intervals of time during this age. All these new species of animal life appeared suddenly in the fossil record fully formed. There are no indications that one species slowly evolved into another species. This strongly supports the premise that each of these animal species were carefully planned by the amazing Architect and were created by the Amazing Creator according to a preconceived plan. See Figures 1-1 & 1-4.

The fossil record verifies that many hundreds of new animal species of micro and macro size were created during the Fourth Creation Day. Each animal species also relates directly to one of the 35 or so body plans that were established by the Creator during the Lower Cambrian Explosion of Animal Life.

In Conclusion

The Fourth Day was a time of dramatic change in the plant and animal environment throughout the Earth. An abidingly homogeneous, moderate climate of the Third Day was changed by God into a climate that was more dominantly seasonal, changing, harsh and erratic. Plant and animal life which depended on the previous moderate and moist conditions for the most part vanished. God was now preparing the Earth for the Fifth Creation Day.

The Fourth Day saw the initial breakage of the one large continent that was formerly called Pangaea. See Figure 4-2. This resulted in many long linear rift basins to form where great thicknesses of Permian sediments were deposited. The deep seated stress within the earth's crust also caused the Appalachian Mountains to form along the east coast of America and other mountains to form in other parts of the Earth.

Multiple new species of invertebrate life came into being. New species of amphibians and new species of reptiles appeared. All these new species of animal life appeared suddenly in the fossil record fully formed. There are no indications that one species slowly evolved into another species. This strongly supports the premise that each of these animal species were carefully planned by the amazing Architect and were created by the amazing Creator according to a preconceived plan. Each of these new animal species were created to conform with one of the 35 or so phyla (Body Plans) that God established during the time of the Cambrian Explosion of Animal Life. See Figures 1-1 & 1-12.

During the 4th Day, many of the previous species of plant life were replaced with new species of plant life that gave a new face to the plant world. Evolution was not smart enough to do this, but God was. This was the work of the Almighty Architect and Creator of the Universe who brought the 4th

Day to a dramatic close and ushered in a new age that the Bible refers to as the 5th Day.

The great extinctions of plant and animal life at the end of this 4th Day cannot be explained totally on the basis of changes in climate. In fact, climate may not have had anything to do with the majority of the extinctions, but here again the Bible gives a clue. God was in the process of bringing the Paleozoic Era to a close, and was about to usher in a new age called the Fifth Day or in geological terms, the Mesozoic Era. See Figure 1-1.

In other words, there was a divine intervention by God, whereby He brought the Fourth Day to a close and ushered in a new day that is called the Fifth Creation Day. The ending of the Fourth Day included the selective extinction of multiple species of plant and animal life. These changes can be observed in the geological record.

Geologists have for many years observed these changes in the rocks, and have deemed it appropriate to end the Permian on the basis of the selective extinctions of plant and animal life, and to usher in the Triassic, which contains entirely new assemblages of animal and plant life.

Creation Science persons contend that the great volumes of sediments that were deposited during the Fourth Day were deposited by Noah's Flood. This is definitely not the case. They were all deposited in a normal, mappable manner. The question is this: can the geological formations that we have just described be classified under the banner of Uniformitarianism as Creation Science people suggest? Definitely not. Can evolution explain these phenomenal changes, the mass extinctions of life followed by multiple new creations of life? Definitely not.

The 4th Day ended with massive extinctions of animal life. It is conjectured that possibly 98+% of all invertebrate animal life became extinct. 75% of amphibian groups and 80% of reptile groups became extinct. This was truly the dramatic termination of the Paleozoic Era and of the 4th Creation Day.

Let us now open the next geological window to see the exciting new developments that took place during the Fifth Day of Creation. This new age equates to the Mesozoic Era. See Figure 1-1.

References for the 4th Day

1. Campbell G. Morgan, "The Analyzed Bible," p.22.
2. Beasley Walter, F.R.G.S., "AMAZING ARCHITECT," Marshall, Morgan, & Scott, Ltd., London & Edinburgh, 1955, p.101.
3. Carl 0. Dunbar and Karl M. Waage, *Historical Geology*, Third Edition (New York: John Wiley and Sons, Inc., 1969, p.272. Emphasis added.
4. Dunbar and Waage, p. 302-04.
5. Dunbar and Waage, p. 304.
6. Dunbar and Waage, p. 286.
7. Dunbar and Waage, p. 288.
8. I. W. Howchin, The Building of Australia, Part 1, p. 174. (Quotation found in Walter Beasley's book on p.98.)
9. Dunbar and Waage, p. 306.
10. Dunbar and Waage, p. 307.
11. Dunbar and Waage, p. 311.
12. Clark and Stearn, "Geological Evolution of North America," Second Edition, 1968, The Ronald Press Company, USA, p. 459.
13. N. M. Newell, "Crises in the History of Life," Scientific American, Vol. 208, No.2, 1963, p. 79.
14. Dunbar and Waage, p.312.

Note: The primary purpose of this manuscript is not to go into great detail, but to show the astounding relationship that exists between the Record of Geology and the Record of the Bible. The above descriptions have been a part of my lecture series over a period of many years.

Chapter 5

The Fifth Day of Creation

Introduction

On this day God created great water creatures, reptiles such as dinosaurs, winged things and birds that flew above the Earth. When relating this scenario to the geological history of the Earth, one naturally thinks of the Mesozoic Era.

The 98+% of invertebrate species that were abundant during the previous Fourth Day mysteriously disappeared. They were replaced by entirely new invertebrate species. Invertebrate paleontologists have been astounded by this dramatic change.

The Fifth Day relates to the geological Mesozoic Era. This Era is subdivided into time periods called the Triassic, the Jurassic and the Cretaceous Periods. See Figure 1-1.

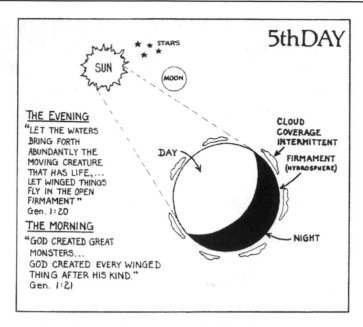

Figure 5-1: An illustration of the Biblical 5th Day of Creation

The Bible Record

The Fifth Day of Creation is recorded as follows in Genesis 1:20-23 (New American Standard Bible) "*20Then God said, "Let the waters teem with swarms of living creatures, and let birds fly above the earth in the open expanse of the heavens. 21God created the **great sea monsters** and every living creature that moves, with which the waters swarmed after their kind, and **every winged bird** after its kind; and God saw that it was good. 22God blessed them, saying, "Be fruitful and multiply, and fill the waters in the seas, and let birds multiply on the earth." 23There was evening and there was morning, a fifth day."*

The Bible says: "*Let the waters teem with swarms of the living creatures,*" (Genesis 1:20, NIV). This means that God was about to create entirely new species of water life. This would include invertebrate and vertebrate animal life that was more comfortable in a water environment than on land.

The science of geology has confirmed the presence of many new species of land plants during the Fifth Day, and similarly, geology has determined that many new strange species of animal life were created during the Fifth Day that were more comfortable in water then they were on land. However, many of this strange marine type of animal life were also able to survive on land as well as in the water.

The plan conceived in the mind of God is set out as follows: *"And God said, Let the waters bring forth abundantly . . ."* (Genesis 1:20). Verse 21 repeats verse 20 almost word for word; however, it describes work being done in the morning of this day by the Creator as follows: *"And God created great sea monsters . . ."* (Genesis 1:21, KJV). The word "create" describes the work that was performed to fulfill God's plan for the Fifth Day.

Once creation was complete, God looked at what he had created and said *"It was good."* (Genesis 1:21b). The goodness of God's creations is a reflection of God's own pervasive goodness. There is inevitability to this statement as each plant and animal life always satisfies a particular environmental and ecological purpose.

The Bible says that *"God is good"* (Psalm 86:5 and 119:68). Every species of plant and animal life was good for this Earth, and has played a significant role in the development of the Earth. Often these roles have direct and indirect effects. For instance, oil, gas and coal are products of organic life, which were vital living things millions of years ago, and which are being used today to heat homes, generate electricity and operate automobiles, produce plastics, and so forth. The Earth itself has been enriched by the life that was present in the ancient past. Today our personal lives are being enriched by what God has done in the past. Thus, it is important to know what God has done in the past that is benefiting us today.

God pronounced his blessings upon the life that he created on the Fifth Day and commanded that the animal and bird life would be fruitful, and multiply, and that they would fill the waters in the seas and that the winged things would multiply on the Earth (Genesis 1:22).

The Fifth Day of Creation is divided into an evening and a morning. It was in the evening that God the Father came forth with an architectural blueprint or plan for this day. It was in the morning and throughout this day that the Creator performed the work necessary to bring this Fifth Day into reality. See Figures 5-1 and 1-1.

The Geological Record

The actual length of the Fifth Day cannot be established with certainty. According to geology, the Mesozoic Era, which corresponds to the Fifth Day, is now estimated to be about 160 million years in duration. This, of course, is based on available radioactive dating methods and could well be quite accurate. See Figure 1-1.

Another method of determining the relative age of the Mesozoic Era is on the basis of the thickness of stratified sediments. This method isn't very reliable because the rates of sedimentation differ greatly for different kinds of sediments, even for rocks of the same composition. No satisfactory account can be taken of time represented by interruptions of sedimentation, where long periods of non deposition and/or erosion persisted. Nevertheless, one can arrive at something of an estimate. The 160 million year figure stated may be quite plausible.

The thickness of rock sequences represented by the Triassic, Jurassic and Cretaceous vary from place to place. The thicknesses are often 4000 to 6000 feet (1200 to 1800 m) in the more stable platform areas, whereas in the basin areas, the accumulated thicknesses may exceed 20,000 to 30,000 feet (6100 to 9100 m). How is it possible to accurately date these great thicknesses?

The Mesozoic, as well as other geological ages, reveal distinct worldwide cycles of sedimentation. In these cycles, the sea would transgress the land areas and then would regress. There are often multiple transgressions and regressions of shoreline areas. This cyclic characteristic is not a product of a single worldwide flood. Careful examination of these stratigraphic sequences reveals distinctly where old shoreline areas used to exist. In a landward direction one can map the continental deposits characterized by land plants, land animals and coal deposits. In a seaward direction, the deposits are characterized by shoreline beach sands, offshore sand bars and shallow water and fresh water or marine plant and animal life. It is evident that these sediments were deposited slowly, under conditions that were essentially similar to how sedimentary processes are taking place today.

About 60% of the world's oil and 65% of the world's gas reserves are found in sediments of the Fifth Day. Oil and gas are often associated with beach sands and sand bars that relate to the multiple layers of ancient shorelines.

Climate

The climate that prevailed during the latter half of the Fourth Creation Day, or the Middle and Upper Permian, is believed to have continued into and throughout the Fifth Day. Scattered cloud coverage was characteristic of this age, where the sun was free to shine directly upon the face of the Earth (See Figure 5-1). The moon and stars would have been clearly visible from the surface of the Earth at night.

The average temperatures of the Fifth Day, the Mesozoic Era, were significantly warmer than today. There were no evidences of glaciers or ice in any parts of the Earth. Cesate Emillard[1] implied that "*mean temperatures probably exceeded 10ºC, even in the Polar Regions, as ocean bottom temperatures have not been recorded lower than 14ºC from sediments deposited during this time.*" According to Newell[2] "*There is an absence of coral reefs in polar regions, and a widespread distribution in equatorial zones, which indicates polar temperatures were somewhat lower than 20ºC, and equatorial temperatures were around 29ºC for this period of time.*" This is the period of time that relates to the Fifth Day.

The Great Reptiles and Winged Things

The Bible directs our attention to three areas of creation during the 5th Day which can be directly related to the geological history of the Earth. We read in Genesis 1:20-23 (New American Standard Bible) "*²⁰Then God said, "Let the waters teem with swarms of living creatures, and let birds fly above the earth in the open expanse of the heavens." ²¹God created the **great sea monsters** and **every living creature** that moves, with which the waters swarmed after their kind, and **every winged bird** after its kind; and God saw that it was good. ²²God blessed them, saying, "Be fruitful and multiply, and fill the waters in the seas, and let birds multiply on the earth." ²³There was evening and there was morning, a fifth day.*"

Firstly, God created great water monsters which can be related to the dinosaurs, the so-called "terrible lizards." Secondly, God created every living creature that moves with which the waters brought forth abundantly, (Genesis 1:21 KJV), which can be related to the marine reptiles (i.e. the Plesiosaurs). It can also apply to the many new species of invertebrate life and to other new species of sea life. Thirdly, God created winged things that fly in the open firmament of heaven. (Genesis 1:20b) This can be related to the birds and flying reptiles (See Figures 1-1 and 5-2 and 5-3).

Dinosaurs: The Great Water Monsters

The Bible directs our attention to the creatures that were created during the Fifth Day. Clues are given as to what they were like. They were creatures that the waters brought forth (Genesis 1:21).

Beasly[3] says, *"The word "whale" is a misnomer, for the Hebrew word taniniym can be translated as "monster" and as "a long drawn out thing."* When the English scholars were translating the Hebrew word tanniynim, the largest water animal that they knew about was the whale, because they didn't have access to the fossil record and the knowledge of the dinosaurs. Dr. W. Bennett[4] says, *"tanniynim, translated "monsters," can be explained "as a long, thin, stretched-out thing, like a serpent."* By relating this translation to the known vertebrates, one can see that the great Giant Lizards or Dinosaurs of the Mesozoic Era fit the Biblical description in a most remarkable way. The reconstruction of a Jurassic Sauropod dinosaur "Apatosaurus," bears a remarkable resemblance to this description. See Figure 5-2. It was a long, thin, stretched-out thing like a serpent.

Many of the dinosaurs lived on land, but it is also evident that even these creatures were quite comfortable in water. Thus, they could be described as water monsters; likened, perhaps, to present-day crocodiles and alligators that can live on the land, but are also at home in the water.

An analysis of geological evidence reveals that an inland sea extended northward from the Gulf of Mexico and southward from the Arctic Ocean throughout the central and western portions of the United States and Canada during much of

Mesozoic time. The dinosaurs would have had easy access to waters of this inland sea. This inland sea was bordered by a shoreline to the west where the present Canadian Rocky Mountains and the equivalent mountains to the south in the USA are today present. These mountains did not form until after the dinosaurs became extinct. This western shoreline provided opportunities for the dinosaurs to walk on to the land areas and to eat the lush vegetation that was present onshore.

Land Dinosaurs

The Earth Sciences reveal that multi species of animal life occupied every continent on Earth. The global climate was relatively warm. There are no evidences of glacial ice anywhere throughout the Earth.

Dinosaur Provincial Park and other areas in southern Alberta, Canada has yielded hundreds of partial and complete skeletons from the Cretaceous period. These skeletons are on display at the Royal Tyrrell Museum of Paleontology located at Drumheller, Alberta, Canada.

Dinosaurs were present on Earth during much of the Mesozoic Era. They appeared during the late Triassic Period and flourished during the Jurassic and Cretaceous times. Climate changes enabled these creatures to feed and thrive on the lush growth of vegetation near rivers and bodies of water.

Fossil records of the late Triassic period reveal the first dinosaurs. Examples are the small Saltopus (a small cat-sized meat-eater), as well as one of the largest dinosaurs of that period, the Plateosaurus. This plant-eater measured about 25 feet (8m) in length and was tall enough to reach and eat leaves on trees. These are only two of the many dinosaur fossils that have been found and reconstructed.

During the Jurassic Period dinosaurs of enormous sizes appeared. Best known are the Sauropods like the giant Brachiosaurus and Diplodicus which fed on the abundant plants that flourished in the warm, moist climate of this period. Some of these giant dinosaurs grew to be *up to 90 feet (25m) in* length. They were thought to be as at home in the water as on land, often hiding in the deep waters to escape their enemies, with only their eyes and nostrils above the water. Stegosaurus, the armor-plated plant eater also lived during the Jurassic. Of the meat-eaters living during this period, the fierce Megalosaurus and Allosaurus are best known. Smaller fast-running raptors like Velociraptor were present during the Jurassic.

Some of the Jurassic Dinosaurs lived on into the Cretaceous Period; however, many new ones appeared in the fossil record. Of note are the Tyrannosaurus Rex and the Albertosaurus which are called "tyrant lizards" because of their ability to move fast to capture their prey. The duck-billed Corythosaurus, the Iguanodon, Edmontosaurus and other plant-eaters were often prey for Tyrannosaurus. Also living during the Cretaceous time was Triceratops, best known of the horned dinosaurs, and Ankylosaurus the armor-plated dinosaur. Struthiomimus was an ostrich-like dinosaur that raided the nests of other dinosaurs and stole their eggs.

Visitors to the Royal Tyrrell Museum, at Drumheller, Alberta are impressed with the variety, sizes and shapes of the many dinosaurs which are on display. Many of these were excavated from the Cretaceous formations called "the badlands" at Dinosaur Provincial Park (now a UNESCO World Heritage Site), located about 175 km (110 miles) away from Calgary. Dr. Philip Currie, Curator of Dinosaurs at the Royal Tyrrell Museum of Paleontology at Drumheller says, "*Some thirty-eight species of more than thirty-four genera of twelve families of dinosaurs have been found here, along with the fossil remains of many varieties of fish, turtles, marsupials, and amphibians."*[5]

It is believed that most dinosaurs were egg-laying, similar to modern day reptiles, and that their young were hatched from eggs laid in nests. Evidence of this is based upon an important fossil discovery by Roy Chapman in the Mongolian desert, which is recorded by Clark and Stearn[6] who say, *"Skeletons of the primitive ceratopsian "Protoceratops" were found associated with clutches of eggs and immature specimens. In some of the elongate eggs, laid to hatch in the warmth of the sun 100 million years ago, the remains of embryonic dinosaurs could be detected. Although dinosaur eggs are among the rarest of fossils, such finds as the Mongolian one leave little doubt that dinosaurs reproduced in this manner."*

Dr. Philip Currie led a team that made a similar discovery of dinosaur eggs in Southern Alberta in 1997. Not only did they find eggs and baby dinosaur bones, they also found eggs with dinosaur embryos in them. Lisa Murphy-Lamb[7], who writes about this amazing discovery of nests of eggs states, *"Philip's finds were evidence of a new species, Hypacrosaurus stebingeri, which was a large, bipedal high-crested hadrosaur measuring about eight metres long."*

By the end of the Cretaceous Age all of these many species of dinosaurs had become extinct. What caused their extinction?

Figure 5-2: Apatosaurus, a Jurassic Sauropod that inhabited North America during the Fifth Day. Art work by Elaine Daae.

The Marine Reptiles

There were three groups of marine reptiles; the plesiosaurs, mosasaurs and ichthyosaurs, that spent their entire life in the water. They all attained great lengths, and had one special feature, a very rapid seal-like movement through the water. They were predatory carnivores that fed mostly on fish. There were many species of each and they all became extinct by the end of the Cretaceous Age. Why did they mysteriously become extinct worldwide?

The Plesiosaurs: had a small head, a long, flexible neck, a short, thick body and a relatively short tail. Beasley[8] says, *"They propelled themselves gracefully through the water by means of large, powerful, paddle-like flippers. About 100 different species of plesiosaur have been found in various parts of the world, differing in length from 3 to 50 feet (1 to 15 meters)"* (see Figure 5-3).

The Ichthyosaurs: were shark-like in appearance, with a long jaw armed with many sharp teeth for catching fish. Swinton and Pinner[9] say, *"Well preserved skeletons with embryonic young within the body cavity suggest that these animals did not lay eggs but bore their young in the ocean as do the whales."* The largest ichthyosaurs grew to 30 feet (9.12m), but many were only 5 to 6 feet (1.5 to 1.8m) long.

The Mosasaurs: were marine, lizard-like creatures that are only found in rocks of Cretaceous age. Moore[10] says, *"The head was long and pointed, the body slender, the tail flattened, and the limbs paddle-shaped. Some species attained a length of about 40 feet (12.2m)."*

Is it possible that the Bible is directing our attention to the swimming marine reptiles that spent all of their time in the water, similar to the sharks and fish, which is recorded as follows: [21] *"And God created every living creature that moveth which the waters brought forth abundantly, after its kind"* (Genesis 1:21,KJV).

Beasley[11] says, *"The word "moveth" is derived from the Hebrew word ramas, and it means to "move lightly," to "glide about," or to "glide with the swift movement of a fish."* The word "abundantly" is from the Hebrew word *sherets*, and it means to "swarm with swarms.

The Bible portrays a picture during the Fifth Day of the sea being literally swarming with great numbers of creatures that glide about with the swift movement of fish. It would appear that the marine reptiles and the great water monsters are grouped together in the following verse, *"God said, "Let the waters teem with swarms of living creatures, and let birds fly above the earth in the open expanse of the heavens."* (Genesis 1:20, New American Standard Bible). Here we have the words to describe all of the water creatures, implying that the waters were teeming with swarms of these swiftly gliding creatures of both land and marine forms of reptiles.

Pterosaurs and Birds: Winged Things That Fly

The pterosaurs are the flying reptiles that first appeared during the Lower Jurassic. Like the dinosaurs, the pterosaurs developed into giants, the largest with a wing spread of more than 25 feet (7.6m), although the body was only the size of a turkey. This was the largest animal, in terms of wing span, ever to fly. They had sharp, slender teeth, and heads that were decidedly reptilian. During the Jurassic Period, the pterosaurs ranged in size from minute species with a wingspread equal to that of a sparrow up to others with a wingspread of 3 or 4 feet (1-1.3m). The larger species are found exclusively in rocks of the Cretaceous.

Clark and Stearn[12], say, *"The first bird appeared as a fossil during the Upper Jurassic and was given the name Archaeopteryx (Gr. archaios; ancient and pteron; wing)."* It was found as a complete skeleton with impressions of feathers clearly preserved. This discovery was found in the lithographic limestone quarry at Solenhofen, Germany. Two other specimens of Archaeopteryx about the size of a crow have also been found.

Archaeopteryx is classified as a bird because it had feathers. Otherwise it might well have been classified as a reptile, having many reptilian characteristics. For instance, it had rows of small, sharp conical teeth, set in individual sockets in its long bill. The bones of the wing are not birdlike: the four digits were not completely fused, and the first three functioned as claws. As well, the tail has a long axis composed of separate vertebrae with the feathers diverging pinnately from its axis, and not fanlike as in modern birds.

Figure 5-3: A western North American seascape of the Late Cretaceous; including the mosasaurs tylosaurus attacked by the pterosaurs with pteranodon, the largest of the pterosaurs overhead. Artwork by Elaine Daae.

Hesperornis, known by complete skeletons and by impressions of its feathers in the fine-textured Upper Cretaceous Niobrara Chalk of Kansas, was a large swimming and diving bird. Dunbar and Waage[13] say, *"It resembled a penguin and its stretched out length was about 6 feet (1.83 m). It also had sharp, slightly recurved reptilian teeth in its long bill. The feet were webbed, and it had long, strong, powerful legs for swimming."*

Moore[14] says, *"Another bird called Ichtyornis resembled modern sea gulls, and had well-developed, strong wings."* Dunbar & Waage[15] say, *"Several of our modern birds also lived during the Cretaceous, such as ducks, grebes and pelicans."*

There are presently 16 groups of modern birds and 14 of these groups had their beginnings during the Cretaceous Period which equates to the Fifth Creation Day. This once again confirms the complete accuracy of the Biblical Record as it relates to the Geological Record.

The Bible says that during the Fifth Day, God created winged things that fly. Beasley[16] comments on this interesting phrase as follows: *"Notice particularly that the sacred writer did not say, 'Let birds fly' but rather 'let flying things fly.' It is true that birds did fly in this era, and this statement, if used, would have been correct but not complete. It was necessary to use words which would include other flying creatures besides birds, such as the Pterodactyls (flying reptiles)."*

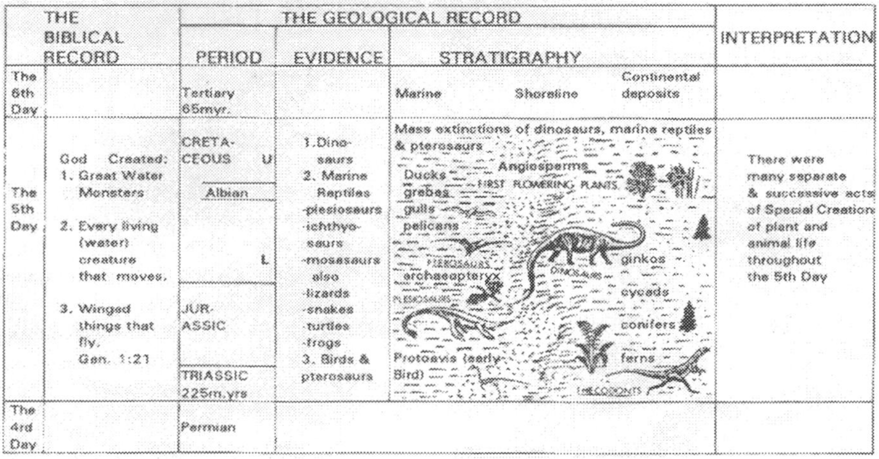

Figure 5-4: Compares the 5th Day to the geological Cretaceous, Jurassic and Triassic Periods. These sediments are generally several thousand feet thick. In the great basin regions they are up to 20,000 + feet (4,572m) in thickness. It reveals when the various plant & animal species first appeared. Figure by Don Daae.

This again shows the complete accuracy of the scriptures, which can be trusted in their minutest detail. The phrase,

"Let winged things fly" refers to the flying reptiles as well as the birds.

Raschi [Rabbi Solomon Ben Isaac],[17] who lived between 1040 and 1105 A.D., states in his Bible commentary to Genesis that the Hebrew word oaf, often translated "fowl," is not exclusive to fowl, but rather includes things like flies as well. In effect, oaf has a broader meaning than "fowl," and also according to Beasley, it can be interpreted as "flying things" in general.

The First True Bird

The first true bird appeared during the Lower Triassic Age. See Figure 5-4. It was called Protoavis texensis.

Protoavis texensis was discovered in a mudstone quarry in Texas by Sankar Chatterjee.[18] He was a paleontologist from Texas Tech University. When he found the fossil bones in 1983, he imagined they were just some baby dinosaur fossils. They were put into storage until 1985, when upon analysis he began to realize the significance of his find. In June, 1991, he released details of his discovery in the Philosophical Transactions of the Royal Society of London, "*Cranial Anatomy and Relationships of a new Triassic Bird from Texas.*"[17]

Chatterjee calls this first bird, "*Protoavis texensis.*" It was about the size of a pheasant, counting its long bony tail. He points out that the skeleton shows further bird characteristics such as a wishbone, a shoulder modified for flying, and a keeled sternum, which serves as an attachment point for flight muscles on most birds.

It was a true bird in that it had a full plumage of feathers. The fact that birds do have anatomical similarities to reptiles, and that both reptiles and birds reproduce by the laying of eggs, is often cited by evolutionists to support the idea that birds evolved from the thecodont reptiles. This argument is of limited convenience, however, as other basic differences exist. In particular, birds are "warm blooded," that is, they have the ability to maintain their body at a constant temperature; whereas reptiles are "cold blooded," which means that their body temperature is determined by the temperature of the surrounding air.

Marine Invertebrate Life

The previous Fourth Day ended with massive extinctions of 98%+ of Paleozoic invertebrate life. The Fifth Day began with the emergence of completely new species of invertebrate life. This is one of the reasons why geologists and paleontologist are able to differentiate the sediments of Permian Age from the overlying Triassic, Jurassic and Cretaceous Age sediments. See Figure 1-1.

The Ammonoids: It is said that the Triassic sea swarmed with ammonoids. Dunbar & Waage[19] say. "*They were not only the most beautiful and characteristic shelled animals of the Mesozoic seas, but they have also proved to be the most useful marine invertebrates for defining the fossil zones used in correlation of strata. The entire Mesozoic is zoned on the basis of ammonoids.*"

Dunbar & Waage[20] describe the history of the Ammonoids. They say, "*The ammonoids suffered great exterminations three times—at the end of the Devonian Period, at the end of the Permian and at the end of the Triassic. Each time a few survived to start another great radiation; however, they failed to survive a fourth great decline and at the end of the Cretaceous Period became totally extinct.*" This equates to the end of the Fifth Day. See Figure 1-1. Why did they become extinct?

Reef Building Corals: Many modern reef building species of corals appeared during the Triassic Period. Many thick limestone reef formations throughout Europe, Asia, the Americas and other parts of the Earth were deposited at this time.

Many new species of brachiopods, pelecypods, cephalopods, crustacean and other invertebrate animal phyla also came into existence during the Triassic, Jurassic and Cretaceous Periods at different intervals of time.

Mesozoic Plants

Cycads: The Mesozoic Era, in terms of plant life, maybe called the "Age of Cycadophytes," because cycad plants, which are unimportant today, were the dominant trees of the Triassic, Jurassic and Lower Cretaceous. Thereafter they declined rapidly.

Cycads are gymnosperms and are palm-like in appearance. They have a woody trunk with a large central pith cavity, and the outer part bearing closely spaced pitted scars that mark the place of former attachments of the leaves. The trunk is very short and bulbous in some species; about as wide as high, but in others it attains a height of more than 50 feet (15.2m). At the top is a graceful crown of long, palm-like leaves which have a strong stem axis, and very numerous, elongate leaflets on the two sides.

Cycads began during the Permian and reached their maximum development during the Jurassic. Two-thirds of the known plant fossils of this age are of this type. The cycads include two distinct groups; one became extinct in Cretaceous time, whereas a few genera of the other group survive today in warm regions.

Conifers: The conifer is a gymnosperm, and this plant group includes the pines, cedars and other cone-bearing evergreens. Conifers first appeared at the end of the Pennsylvanian, and continued through the Permian and flourished as an important group in the flora of the Mesozoic. The average diameter of some of the trees was 3 to 4 feet (0.9 to 1.2 m) with a height of 60 to 80 feet (18 to 24 m). Some logs 7 feet (2.1 m) in diameter and 125 feet (38 m) in length have been observed. There were several kinds of Sequoia trees, some very much like the giant sequoia (redwoods) of California, and a number of species belonging to the cypress, yew, cedar and juniper types. Most of these conifer plant groups have continued to the present.

Ginkgos: The ginkgo is a gymnosperm. It was present during the previous Permian Age. It is one of the more interesting fossil plants from a botanical standpoint, because it was one of the most abundant and widely distributed trees during Jurassic time and is represented today by a single species, native in China and Japan. The present day ginkgo attains a height of 80 feet (24.4m) or more, it has a relatively smooth trunk that may be up to 3 feet (1 m) in diameter. It bears broad, sub triangular leaves with veins radiating from the pointed base.

Ferns: Ferns comprise about one-third of the known floras of the Mesozoic, and they experienced a sharp decline in number during the Upper Cretaceous. The ferns which propagated by seed became extinct at the end of the Jurassic, whereas the spore bearing ferns continued right through to the present day. Many of the smaller shrubs acted as filler plants, whereas other species were fairly large trees.

Horsetails: The horsetails trace their ancestry back to the Devonian. The group known as calamites became extinct during the Triassic. The ribbed stems were 20 to 30 feet (6.0-9.1m) long and 4 to 5 inches (10-13 cm) in diameter. However, some of the smaller horsetail species have continued to the present day.

Angiosperms: The First Flowering Plants

The sudden emergence of the Angiosperms towards the end of the Lower Cretaceous is one of the most outstanding developments in the history of plant life. It is totally amazing. See Figure 1-1.

An angiosperm is any vascular plant of the phylum or division Anthophyta. They have seeds enclosed in a fruit, grain, pod, or capsule. They comprise all flowering plants. For example, peas are enclosed in a pod, or pear seeds are enclosed within the fruit. This is in contrast to the Gymnosperms, which means "naked seed," where the seed is borne exposed, as on the woody scales of a pine cone.

There are two classes of angiosperms, monocotyledons and dicotyledons. The former include the grasses, cereals, palms, lilies, etc., the latter contain the deciduous trees, such as maples, oak, elm, and a great variety of shrubs and herbs. Lee McAlester[21] reports that angiosperms today *"overwhelmingly dominate the land. Of the 260,000 or so living species of vascular plants, about 250,000 or 96% are angiosperms; the other 10,000 species are mostly ferns, whereas gymnosperms, despite wide distribution and local importance have only 700 surviving species."*

The Cretaceous is divided into two time subdivisions called the Lower and Upper Cretaceous, which in turn are each divided into smaller time units or epochs such as the Aptian, Albian, Cenomanian, Turonian, etc. It was during the **Upper Albian Epoch that the first flowering plants suddenly appeared.** Among the oldest of these were the magnolia, fig, sassafras and poplar, together with some of the seed and fruit bearing shrubs, annuals and some of our common vegetables. See Figure 1-1.

By the beginning of the Upper Cretaceous (Cenomanian Age), the forests were essentially modern, including such trees as the beeches, birches, maples, oaks, walnuts, plane trees, tulips, sweet gums, breadfruit, and ebony, along with shrubs like the laurel, ivy, hazel-nut, and holly.

The dramatic, sudden appearance of angiosperms on every continent during the Upper Albian is mystifying to the evolutionist, as Lee McAlester[22] relates, "*One of the most perplexing problems in the entire evolutionary record of plants concerns the origin of the angiosperms. Scattered fossil fragments that may represent angiosperms are occasionally found in Triassic and Jurassic rocks, but the certain record of the group begins suddenly in Lower Cretaceous deposits. Moreover, many of the major angiosperm subgroups are already differentiated when they first appear in the fossil record. This fact suggests that the group had a considerable pre-Cretaceous history that, for some reason, is not recorded in the fossil record. Perhaps these earlier angiosperms are unknown because they were rare and local in occurrence, or were confined to highland areas where erosion was active and fossilization unlikely. In any case, there are no transitional fossils to indicate the ancestry of the group. Possibly they originated from the seed-ferns or from some other group of gymnosperms, but some botanists think they may have evolved directly from seedless ancestors.*" In other words, the only logical explanation is that they were specially planned and created by the amazing Architect and Creator of the universe. There are no evidences of one plant species ever evolving into another plant species.

Evolutionist charts always show a root projecting down from the Albian Epoch indicating that the angiosperms are somehow related to some previous plant life, but no transitional forms are in evidence. If evolution was a fact, then there would be multi ancestral plant species. This again gives strong support to the fact that they were created by an Almighty Creator God. See Figure 1-1 and Figure 5-4.

The Bible is silent as to the creation of the angiosperms during the Fifth Day, but once again, this is an illustration of Psalm 85:11 which says, *"Truth shall spring out of the earth."* Where the Bible is silent, the Earth speaks. The Earth sciences reveal the thousands of different species of angiosperms, their size, shape and the approximate time during the Fifth Day that they first appeared. The angiosperms have continued to flourish to the present. The fact that each species appeared suddenly with no ancestors is strong evidence that they were specially created by the amazing Creator God. The geological record reveals that all our present day species were not created at one time, but that there were literally thousands of successive acts of special creation. Each time unit has a unique assemblage of plant and animal life which distinguishes it from every other unit.

An analysis of plant and animal life throughout the geological history of the Earth reveals that, as a rule, new plant life always precedes a new form of animal life. For example, the marine plant life (algae together with bacteria) of the Proterozoic Age preceded the creation of marine animal life (invertebrates) during the Cambrian Explosion of Animal Life. The ferns and gymnosperms were the first land plants created during the Upper Silurian and Devonian Periods. They preceded the first land animals (amphibians) that appeared during the Upper Devonian. The gymnosperms of the Permian Age preceded the giant dinosaurs and other reptiles of the Mesozoic Era. The angiosperms (true flowering plants) of the Albian & Upper Cretaceous preceded the warm blooded mammals of the Cenozoic.

The Earth was being prepared by God during the latter part of the Fifth Day via the creation of the true flowering plants called angiosperms in preparation for the creation of the warm blooded animals. Mammals are highly dependent upon the grasses, cereals, and all the angiosperm plants for food. Truly, God has always prepared the Earth with proper food for the animal life that He creates.

Earth's First Mammals

The Earth sciences reveal the sudden appearance of two main orders of warm blooded mammals during the latter part of the Fifth Day. They are the placental insectivores and the pouch-bearing marsupials of the Upper Cretaceous. This is historic because they are the two first orders of warm blooded animals to appear on planet Earth. See figure 6-2.

Insectivores: Only teeth and jaw bones have been found in Upper Cretaceous sediments. They were all small, about the size of a rat or a rabbit, and were relatively few in number. These insectivores were placental mammals and resembled modern day shrews, moles and hedgehogs. Figure 6-2 illustrates how certain new species of this Insectivore Order have continued to survive to the present day.

Marsupials: Clarke & Stearn[23] say, "*Marsupials and placental mammals first appear in the Upper Cretaceous rocks. Both groups reached their greatest development in the Cenozoic Era.*"

These two above mentioned mammals first appeared during the latter part of the Cretaceous Period.

It is interesting to note that it wasn't until the Sixth Creation Day or the Tertiary Period, that the additional "Thirteen Major Orders" of warm blooded mammals made their first appearance. See Figures 1-1, 5-4, 6-2.

The End of the Fifth Day

The end of the Mesozoic Era equates to the end of the Fifth Day of Creation. See Figure 1-1. It was a time of massive extinctions of many animal species. Dunbar & Waage[24] says, *"The end of the Cretaceous like the end of the Paleozoic, proved to be a great crisis in the history of life, several stocks of animals declined markedly during the period; others till near its end only to become extinct."*

Dunbar & Waage[25] go on to say, *"For example, the dinosaurs were highly varied and apparently adaptive right up to the end of the Cretaceous time, yet not one is known to have lived to see the dawn of the Cenozoic Era. The pterosaurs specialized perhaps too far, attaining their great size only to die out considerably before the close of the period. Among the great marine reptiles, the ichthyosaurs and plesiosaurs were already on a marked decline, while the mosasaurs underwent a meteoric evolution, yet all these died out and only the marine turtles survived."*

With respect to the invertebrate species, Dunbar & Waage[26] say *"The decline and extinction of the ammonoids and belemnites at the very close of the period, and the passing of the reef-dwelling rudist bivalves and other very common Cretaceous Groups like the exogyras, gryphea, and inoceramids show that the marine invertebrates did not escape the crisis. Indeed a close survey of many invertebrate groups would reveal that a number of common Mesozoic stocks became extinct."* This extraordinary extinction of invertebrate life took place just prior to or at the end of the Fifth Day of Creation.

Indeed each of the above mentioned invertebrate species of animal life can be related directly to one of the 35 or so body plans or Phyla that were created and established by the Creator of the Universe at the time of the Cambrian Explosion of Animal Life. See Figure 1-12.

The amazing compatibility that exists between the Geological Record and the Bible Record is revealed in this Chapter. Every new species of plant and animal life that has been discovered through the geological sciences was designed, created, formed and made for a definite ecological purpose.

The geological faunal break separating the rocks of this age from the next geological age is very sharp. The end of the Mesozoic is marked by the sudden and dramatic selective extinctions of land and marine animal life. The great dinosaurs, pterosaurs and the marine reptiles (plesiosaurs, ichthyosaurs and mosasaurs) suddenly became extinct, whereas certain species of turtles, lizards, snakes and crocodiles continued to survive into the Tertiary Period of the Sixth Day.

There were also selective extinctions among the marine invertebrates such as the belemnites, reef building rudist bivalves, as well as common Cretaceous invertebrate groups such as gryphaea, inoceramids, and exogyras. A closer analysis reveals that a number of Mesozoic species of foraminifera became extinct at this time.

The selective extinction of certain groups and species of animal life is very difficult to explain, because other groups and species continued through without any affect. The great number of fish, the land plants, and corals were basically unaffected.

It is important to note that the body plans of every new species of animal life, micro and macro, that appeared during this Fifth Day of Creation relate directly to one of the 35 or so Phyla (body plans) that were established during the Cambrian Explosion of Animal Life. See Figure 1-12. This again reveals the amazing plan that our Great Divine Architect and Creator God had established in advance for this geological Era. See Figures 1-1 and 1-3.

God brought the Fifth Day to a dramatic close and ushered in a new age called the Sixth Day. We now have geological evidence to verify that this age was terminated by a worldwide cataclysmic event. This event will be described as it relates to the beginning of the Sixth Day. Let us now investigate the Sixth Creation Day to see how it relates to the geological record which is referred to as the Cenozoic Era. This next age is also referred to as the age of the warm blooded mammals.

References for the 5th Day

1. Cesate Emillard, "Cenozoic Climate Changes as indicated by the Stratigraphy and Chronology of Deep Sea Cores of Globigerina Ooze Facies." New York Academy of Science Annals, 1961, Vol. 95, pp. 531-536. Seep.98
2. Norman D. Newell, "Evolution of Reefs" Scientific American, Vol. 226, No. 6, 1972, pp. 54-65.
3. Beasley Walter, F.R.G.S., "Creation's Amazing Architect," Marshall, Morgan, & Scott, Ltd., London & Edinburgh, 1955, p.101.
4. Bennett W.H., "Genesis" *The Century Bible* 1st edn., p. 81.
5. Currie, Philip J. & and Eva B. Koppelhus, Eds., Dinosaur Provincial Park," Indiana University Press, Bloomington, 2005. Front Jacket.
6. Clark and Stearn, "Geological Evolution of North America," Second Edition, 1968, The Ronald Press Company, USA, p. 474.
7. Murphy Lamb, Lisa, "Dinosaur Hunters," Altitude Publishing Canada Ltd., Canmore AB., 2003, p.111.
8. Beasley, p. 110.
9. Swinton and Pinner, The Corridor of Life (1948), p. 165. This is a reference by Beasley on page 118.

10. Moore, Raymond C., Historical Geology, Mcgraw-Hill Book Company, Inc., New York & London, 1933. p. 478.
11. Beasley, p. 110.
12. Clark and Stearn, p.479.
13. Dunbar and Waage, p. 394.
14. Moore, p. 480.
15. Dunbar and Waage, p. 395.
16. Beasley, p. 111.
17. Raschi [Rabbi Solomon Ben Isaac], Bible commentary to Genesis. (See website www.Raschi Rabbi Ben Isaac, Bible commentary to Genesis.)
18. Sankar Chatterjee, "Cranial Anatomy and relationships of a New Triassic bird from Texas," pp.277-342, June 1991. In the Philosophical Transactions of the Royal Society of London.
19. Dunbar and Waage, p. 338.
20. Dunbar and Waage, p. 338.
21. A. Lee McAlester, "The History of Life." (Prentice-Hall, Inc., Englewood Cliffs, New Jersey), p.97.
22. Lee McAlester, p. 304.
23. Clark & Stearn, p. 483.
24. Dunbar and Waage, p. 398.
25. Dunbar and Waage, p. 398-399.
26. Dunbar and Waage, p. 398-399.

Chapter 6

The Sixth Day of Creation

Introduction

During the Sixth Day God created the beasts of the Earth, cattle, creeping things and man. In the geological history of the Earth, one associates this time with the sudden appearance of warm blooded animals; or more specifically to the age of the warm blooded mammals.

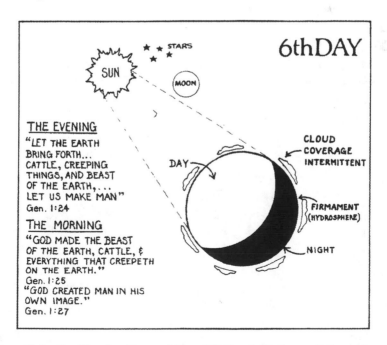

Figure 6-1: An illustration of the Biblical 6th Day of Creation

The History of the Earth chart (Figure 1-1) relates the Sixth Day to the Cenozoic Era. This era is subdivided into time periods called the Tertiary and Quaternary, which are in turn subdivided into smaller time units referred to as epochs. These epochs are named Paleocene, Eocene, Oligocene, Miocene, Pliocene, Pleistocene and Recent by the science of geology. Each of these epochs has a unique record of animal life. The first epoch, the Paleocene, began about 65 million years ago. These time units unravel the history of the warm blooded animals called mammals. It also relates to all the other species of micro and macro animal life that relate to the entire remaining 35 or so phyla (body plans) that are represented throughout this Cenozoic Era.

The Bible Record

The Sixth Day of Creation is recorded in Genesis 1:24-31 (NIV) as follows, "*24And God said, "Let the land produce **(a plan)** living creatures according to their kinds: the livestock, the creatures that move along the ground, and the wild animals, each according to its kind." And it was so. 25 God made the wild animals according to their kinds, the livestock according to their kinds, and all the creatures that move along the ground according to their kinds **(work done).** And God saw that it was good. 26 Then God said, "Let us make mankind in our image, in our likeness **(a plan)**, so that they may rule over the fish in the sea and the birds in the sky, over the livestock and all the wild animals, and over all the creatures that move along the ground." 27 So God created mankind in his own image, in the image of God he created them; male and female he created them **(work done).** 28 God blessed them and said to them, "Be fruitful and increase in number; fill the earth and subdue it. Rule over the fish in the sea and the birds in the sky and over every living creature that moves on the ground."29 Then God said, "I give you every seed-bearing plant on the face of the whole earth and every tree that has fruit with seed in it. They will be yours for food. 30 And to all the beasts of* *the earth and all the birds in the sky and all the creatures that move along the ground—everything that has the breath of life in it—I give every green plant for food." And it was so.* [31] *God saw all that he had made, and it was very good. And there was evening, and there was morning—the sixth day."*

As with the first five creation days, the Sixth Day can be divided into an evening and a morning. The evening was a time when the Great Divine Architect of the universe came forth with a detailed plan for this day. It was in the morning that the work of fulfilling that plan and creating new life according to that plan began by the Great Divine Creator of the universe. This work continued throughout the Sixth Day until everything had been completed.

When the Lord had completed his work on the Sixth Day, He said in Genesis 1:31, *"It was very good."* This goodness is an inevitable reflection of the goodness of God. The consummation of the Sixth Day is indicated by the significant phrase in verse 31, *"And the evening and the morning were the sixth day."*

It was in the evening of the Sixth Day that a detailed plan was outlined by the Great Master Designer and Architect of the Universe. It was in the morning that the Great Divine Creator commenced to carry out this plan. The work of creating every detail of this plan continued throughout this day. When the day was completed, God said, "It was very good." See Appendix C & D for greater clarification.

The Sixth Day of Creation is portrayed in Figure 6-1. It pictures the sun shining directly upon the Earth, similar to the Fifth Day, with scattered cloud coverage in the atmosphere. The Bible describes four groups of new life that were created during the Sixth Day, namely:

> **The Beasts of the Earth:* represent the many new species of warm blooded animals called mammals that belong to the Chordate Phyla.
> **Cattle:* represent the domestic & clean type of mammals that belong to the Chordate Phyla.
> **Everything that Creeps on the Earth:* represents all other macro & micro species of animal life.
> **Man & Woman:* relate to all Human Beings called Homo sapiens.

Everything that creeps on the Earth would include the great numbers of animal species, micro and macro, that directly relate to all the other 34 or so Animal Phyla (body plans) that were established during the Cambrian Explosion of Animal Life. See Figure 1-12.

An imminent British scientist, Simon Conway Morris[1] said this, *"The concept of the phylum is generally taken to be basic to our understanding of animals inasmuch as each of the phyla corresponds to one of the 35 or so basic body plans identified today."* Simon Conway Morris has spent several years at Field, B.C. at the Burgess Shale outcrops analyzing and evaluating the fossils that relate to the Cambrian Explosion of Animal Life. (See Figure 1-12)

The life forms created by God during the Sixth Creation Day were more specifically of a land type for we read, *"Let the Earth bring forth the living creature after his kind"* (vs. 24). This is in contrast to the Fifth Day when God said: *"Let the waters bring forth."* (Genesis 1:20).

It is necessary to go to the science of geology to find out when God created and formed each specific animal species within the above four groups during the Sixth Creation Day. Man and the domestic animal species, such as cattle, were definitely among God's more final acts of creation during the Sixth Day of Creation. See Figure 1-1.

The Geological Record

According to geology, the Cenozoic Era was about 65 million years in duration. This is based upon radiometric methods of dating. An analysis of the corresponding layers of rock strata and their thicknesses in different parts of the world confirms that 65 million years is an appropriate duration of time.

The Cenozoic is divided into two geological time periods called the Tertiary and the Quaternary. See Figure 1-1. The Tertiary is subdivided into five time intervals called epochs: Paleocene, Eocene, Oligocene, Miocene and Pliocene. The Quaternary is subdivided into two time intervals or epochs called the Pleistocene and Recent. Each epoch has a long and a unique assemblage of animal and plant life. This becomes evident once we begin to research the geological record.

In many of the great basin regions of the Earth the accumulated Cenozoic sediments are in the range of 10,000 to 30,000+ feet (3,000m to 9,100+m) in thickness. In North America these basin regions include the Gulf of Mexico, the Mackenzie Delta, the Baffin Bay region and the Gulf of Alaska. These sediments were all deposited in a normal sequential and mappable manner. Every other similar basin region throughout the world has similar thicknesses of mappable sediments and with similar sequences of animal and plant life.

The Gulf of Alaska is a typical example. I have had the privilege of working and analyzing the sediments in this region. Here the offshore sediments of the Paleocene and Eocene are greater than 4,000+feet (1,200+m) thick, the Lower and Middle Oligocene over 15,000 feet (4,500 m), the Upper Oligocene and Miocene about 5,000 feet (1,500 m), and the Pliocene is in the order of 3,000 feet (910 m): giving a total aggregate maximum thickness of about 28,000 feet (8,500 m). The overlying Pleistocene Epoch sediments are greater than 4,000 feet (1,200 m) in thickness in this region.

This gives a total thickness of about 32,000 feet (9,754 m) of Cenozoic Age sediments that relate directly to the 6th Day of Creation. See Figure 1-1.

In the more stable continental platform regions of the Earth these above mentioned sediments are much thinner, as would be expected, being only in the range of a few hundred or thousand feet (meters) thick in places. However, all the other deep basinal regions throughout the world would have similar thicknesses to the Gulf of Alaska.

What Happened to the Dinosaurs?

Dinosaurs were dominant beasts of the Earth right to the end of the Cretaceous Period, when they all suddenly vanished. Why? The birds continued into the Cenozoic Age which relates to the Sixth Day. The fish, the two species of warm blooded animals called Insectivores and Marsupials came through without any problems. What happened to the dinosaurs? The fact is, they mysteriously disappeared.

The K/T Boundary Discovery

The mystery of the sudden disappearance of the dinosaurs is somewhat resolved as we investigate the so called K/T boundary that separates the Mesozoic Era (The Fifth Day) from the Cenozoic Era (The Sixth Day). See Figure 1-1.

It is often said that the most dramatic and in many respects the most puzzling event in the history of life on Earth is the change from the Mesozoic Age of Reptiles to the Tertiary Age of Mammals. Dunbar & Waage[2] say, *"Throughout the long Mesozoic Era—for more than a hundred million years—reptiles completely dominated life on the earth; but at its close their dynasty suddenly collapsed. Turtles, lizards, snakes, and crocodiles survived, but they are small and restricted in their range, and few are aggressive. At the dawn of the Cenozoic Era the dinosaurs were extinct, the pterosaurs had disappeared, and the great marine reptiles were gone."* Then they say, *"Now the way was open for the mammals to begin their conquest of the earth as completely as the reptiles had done in their day. Thus the Cenozoic has well been called "The Age of Mammals."*

This leads to another question, what happened to the dinosaurs and what do we know about the so called K/T boundary? Earth scientists throughout the Earth have been analyzing the chemistry that exists at the K/T boundary. They have discovered that a mysterious chemical called iridium is present worldwide at this boundary.

The famous world renowned, "Tyrrell Dinosaur Museum" at Drumheller Alberta in Western Canada is geologically situated in close proximity to this K/T boundary. This museum has a display featuring the K/T boundary. It reveals a thin whitish grey marker bed that is rich in iridium that separates the underlying Mesozoic (Upper Cretaceous Age) sediments from the overlying younger Cenozoic Tertiary Age sediments. See Figure 1-1.

The Google[3] website says this, *"The **Cretaceous-Tertiary extinction event**, which occurred approximately 65.5 million years ago (Ma), was a large-scale mass extinction of animal and plant species in a geologically short period of time. Widely known as the **K-T extinction event**, it is associated with a geological signature known as the K-T boundary, usually a thin band of sedimentation found in various parts of the world. K is the traditional abbreviation for the Cretaceous Period derived from the German name Kreidezeit, and T is the abbreviation for the Tertiary Period (a historical term for the period of time now covered by the Paleogene and Neogene periods). The event marks the end of the Mesozoic Era and the beginning of the Cenozoic Era [1] with "Tertiary" being discouraged as a formal time or rock unit by the International Commission on Stratigraphy, the*

K-T event is now called the **Cretaceous-Paleogene** *(or* **K-Pg**) **extinction event** *by many researchers.*[2]"

A relatively short distance to the north of the Drumheller Tyrrell Museum in Alberta, Canada is a famous outcrop that exposes this geological event. It reveals the sudden break that separates the underlying Upper Cretaceous sediments from the above Lower Tertiary beds of Paleocene Age. This is a must to see. The Tyrrell Museum is a famous tourist attraction as was mentioned in Chapter 5. It displays one of the most outstanding displays of multi species of dinosaurs large and small. Many of these dinosaur fossils have been retrieved from the Upper Cretaceous sediments that outcrop throughout this region of Western Canada. Other displays are from other regions of the Earth.

I would advise the reader to go to the Tyrrell Museum website at Drumheller, Alberta, Canada to observe the many gigantic and small dinosaur species that have been excavated from the underlying Mesozoic Sediments. They have been marvelously reconstructed in actual size. All of these many dinosaur species were all very much alive prior to the dramatic K/T event that suddenly terminated the Fifth Creation Day. In other words, we now have geological evidence to verify that this geological age, called the Mesozoic Era was terminated by a worldwide cataclysmic event.

The Cenozoic Climate

The generally warm climate that prevailed during the Mesozoic Era (the Fifth Day) continued into the Cenozoic Era (the Sixth Day). The cloud coverage would have been scattered similar to today. However, there are no evidences of ice or glaciers for the major portion of this Era. This would indicate that the climate throughout the Earth was warm and mild. It was conducive to luxuriant growth of vegetation throughout the world. This warmer climate continued to the latter part of the Pliocene Epoch when the first indications of cooler weather in the form of ice first appeared. This cooler weather intensified at the beginning of the Pleistocene Epoch when a fully fledged Ice Age commenced. See Figure 1-1.

Age of Warm Blooded Mammals

Geological and paleontological studies have revealed that the Cenozoic sediments are above the K/T boundary. They relate to the "Age of the Warm Blooded Animals." The fossil record has revealed that there are at least 15 Orders of warm blooded animals called mammals that relate to the Cenozoic Era. Two of these Orders appeared during the latter part of the previous Upper Cretaceous Age. They were the insectivores & the marsupials. Both of these Orders continued throughout the Cenozoic Era to the present. All of the other Orders came into existence during the Tertiary Age which in turn relate to the Paleocene, Eocene, Oligocene, Miocene, Pliocene and the Pleistocene Epochs. Compare Figure 1-1 with Figure 6-2.

Figure 6-2 reveals when the above major orders of warm blooded mammals first appeared and it also shows the relative abundance of species in each order. Each Mammal order is represented by many separate species that had morphological similarities that were characteristic of that particular order.

The insectivores and the marsupials are two warm blooded mammal orders that had their beginning during the latter part of the 5th Day. In these two orders, there were new species that appeared during the 6th Day while other species would suddenly become extinct. It is interesting to note that there are species that represent these two orders today.

Paleontologists have classified these 15+ Major Orders of warm blooded mammals as chordates. A chordate is a warm blooded mammal that has a vertebral column with a notochord. Geology has confirmed that each Mammal Order contains many unique species that appeared suddenly at many different time intervals. The big question arises: were these new species specially designed by the Great Divine Architect of the universe and were they uniquely created by the Great Divine Creator of the universe according to a definite architectural plan? Or is it possible that each new species evolved by an undirected, unintelligent evolutionary chance process called Evolution?

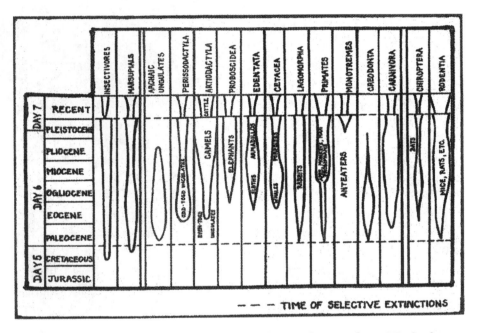

Figure 6-2: This diagram Categorizes the major 15 Orders of Mammals. The width of the above graphics indicates the approximate abundance of species in each Order. Prepared by Don Daae as part of his lecture series. The original data is from A. Lee McAlester's book, "The History of Life."[4]

Darwinists maintain that each new species has come into existence by a mysterious, unintelligent process called Evolution. They always try to prove that every new species must have evolved from a previous species. **After many years of research, they still need to come forth with valid proof.** The evidence that they present is still based upon conjecture and supposition and upon uncertain scientific evidences. They continue to contend that a non intelligent, evolutionary process can do everything. They do this in spite of the fact that they still lack solid evidence of what they are trying to prove. Their scientific authenticity is very suspect.

According to the science of genetics, micro-biology and paleontology etc., each of the mammal species that relate to a specific Order in Figure 6-2 can be related directly to the chordate phyla (body plan) that God created and established at the time of the Cambrian Explosion of Animal Life during the First Creation Day. Figures 1-1 & 1-5. This fact of science has nothing to do with evolution, but it has everything to do with God's creative plan for all later species. **The Cambrian Explosion of Animal Life is an amazing verification that a Creator God exists.**

It is also possible to relate each of these 13+ Orders of mammals with the Biblical "Beasts of the Earth." Each of the vertebrate species that relate to these Orders is a member of the Chordate Phyla (body plan). They are all warm blooded animals. They are all unique to the Cenozoic Era except for the Insectivores and the Marsupials that first appeared during the previous Mesozoic Era. However, new species that relate to the Insectivore and the Marsupial Order have continued to be created by the Creator during the Sixth Day. See Figure 6-2.

Mammals Require Flowering Plants for Food

All warm blooded mammals require flowering plants called angiosperms for food. About 80+% of all flowering plant species called angiosperms appeared suddenly during the previous Albian Epoch that relates to the Fifth Creation Day. This event relates to the mid portion of the Cretaceous Period. See Figure 1-1. This creative event was accomplished by the Creator in preparation for the future appearance of the warm blooded animal species. All mammals depend upon angiosperm plants for their sustenance. This confirms that an intelligent plan was being unveiled in preparation for new species of animal life that would depend upon flowering plants for food.

Up to the Albian Epoch, all species of animal life including the dinosaurs, amphibians and the birds could have survived on the previous types of plant life such as the gymnosperms and water plants, etc. A non-intelligent evolutionary process was definitely not smart enough to foresee the future or to accomplish this great feat, but the Almighty Designer and Creator of the universe was well able to accomplish this remarkable task.

The Two Types of Mammals

There are basically two types of mammals: the placental and the marsupials. They can be further subdivided into 13+ Orders. Thirteen of these groups are classified as placental mammals on Figure 6-2. The offspring of placental mammals develop inside the uterus of the female in a special structure called the placenta, where the young are nourished directly by the mother's body fluids. Marsupial reproduction is different in that the young are born relatively undeveloped. The tiny kangaroo offspring, for instance, crawl into an external pouch where they attach themselves to a mammary nipple and complete their natal development.

Marsupial Mammals

Marsupials make up about 5% of all **Cenozoic** mammals. Lee McAlister[5] says," *During the Late Cretaceous an opossum-type of marsupial was present, however it was not until the Cenozoic that kangaroos, wallabies, koala bears and wombats appeared. The present day Siberian wolf, found in Russia, is a marsupial, and is very similar in external appearance to placental dogs. Wolf-like marsupial carnivores* *were present in South America until Late Cenozoic, and then became extinct."*

The great majority of present day marsupials are found in Australia. In South America the opossum type of marsupials are present. It is interesting to note that many South American marsupial species became extinct by the end of the Pliocene Epoch. It is believed that the marsupials of Australia survived because they were free from the menace of the more voracious predatory mammals. Australia is relatively isolated, and has provided a refuge for these species since Early Cenozoic time. See Figure 1-1.

Placental Mammals

Figure 6-3: Restoration of Coryphodon, an amplypod that belonged to the Archaic Ungulate Order of the Lower Eocene of Wyoming, USA. Redrawn by Elaine Daae from Dunbar & Waage. P.454.

The placental Mammals make up the additional 95% of Cenozoic Mammals. There was a sudden appearance of numerous placental mammals during the Lower Cenozoic. Thirteen plus Orders appeared during the Cenozoic Epoch. The archaic ungulates are represented by the condylarth and amblypod species that first appeared during the Paleocene. The hoofed archaic ungulates became extinct during the Pliocene. see Figure 6-3.

The first rodents are found at the base of the Paleocene. Clark & Stearn[6] say, "*They are the gnawing animals, with four front incisors teeth developed into sharp, chisel edged tools.*" Squirrels are found in Paleocene beds, whereas the group to which rats and mice belong is first represented in Oligocene beds. (See Figure 6-2).

The first Carnivores appeared during the Paleocene, such as the dog family, which is one of the oldest carnivore groups. Clarke & Stearn[7] say, "*The dog family (Canidae) is one of the oldest in the carnivore group, and is one of the few mammalian lineages in which increase in size to gigantism has not occurred. Within the cat family (Felidae) there developed the saber-toothed "tigers" whose upper canine teeth grew to dagger like proportions and projected several inches below the lower jaw when the mouth was closed. The last and largest of the saber-toothed cats was the Late Pleistocene genus Smilodon.*"

Clarke & Stearn[8] also say "One line led to the civets, hyenas, and cats, the other led to the dogs, raccoon, bears and weasels. *A distinct group of living carnivores, known as the pinnipeds, includes the marine seals and walruses.*"

The saber tooth cat, raccoons, bears, and weasels all appeared at a later period of time.

The Elephant Family

The elephant family belongs to the Proboscidea Order (see Figure 6-2). Dunbar & Waage[9] say, "*The first members of this family (the moeitheriums) have been found in rocks of the Late Eocene and Early Oligocene of the Fayum Desert area in Egypt. Another member, phimia, which greatly resembles a modern day elephant except it had a shorter trunk, was found in Early Oligocene beds"*. The giant elephants, called the mastodons, were widely distributed over Europe and Asia during the Miocene, Pliocene and the Pleistocene Epochs. They may have reached North America by the Siberian-Alaskan land bridge in Late Miocene time. Both the four-tusker and shovel-tusker elephants died out in Late Pliocene time, while the two-tusk mastodons continued to live until the end of the Pleistocene Epoch. See Figures 6-2 & 6-4.

Figure 6-4: The Woolly Mammoth was a giant sized elephant. They were dominant during the Pleistocene Ice Age. Drawn by Elaine Daae after Dunbar & Waage.[10]

One of the best known species of the elephant family in North America is the Woolly Mammoth. It lived in the tundra regions surrounding the ice fields, and ranged across both Eurasia and North America during the Pleistocene Epoch. Frozen carcasses found in Siberia show that they bore a thick coat of brownish woolly hair.

Dunbar and Waage[11] say, *"Other species (of elephants) inhabited the warmer regions, particularly the plains of central and southwestern states. One of these, the imperial mammoth of the southwest, attained a height of 14 feet*

(4.3m) at the shoulders and bore tusks as much as 13 feet (3.9m) long. In their present fossil state, a pair of such tusks weighs almost half a ton."

Mastodons have a different tooth pattern from the giant elephants and were believed to be grazers. Mastodons were browsers living more in timbered regions.

Our modern present day elephants did not appear until Late Pleistocene that equates to the Post Wisconsin Age. See Figure 6-5.

The Modern Horse

The modern horse belongs to the odd-toed hoofed mammal often referred to as the Perissodactyla Order (see Figure 6-2). The horse is often portrayed in school textbooks as having evolved beginning with eohippus, a dog size horse with four toes on the front feet, passing via straight-line evolution through three-toed varieties, and ending with the modern one-toed equis. Much of this tale is now known to be incorrect. The development of the horse is more complicated than originally supposed. Gish[12] says: *"To us the family tree of the horse appears to be merely a scenario put together from non-equivalent parts. Nowhere, for example, are there intermediate forms documenting transition from a non-horse ancestor (supposedly a condylarth) with five toes on each foot, to hyracotherium with four toes on the front foot and three on the rear. Neither is there transitional forms between the four-toed Hyracotherium and the three-toed miohippus, or between the latter, equipped with browsing teeth, and the three-toed merychippus, equipped with high-crowned grazing teeth. Finally, the one-toed grazers, such as Equus, appear abruptly with no intermediates showing gradual evolution from the three-toed grazers."*

Gish[13] also says, *"Another name for Eohippus ("dawn horse") is Hyracotherium, which is now believed to have been more like a tapir or a rhinoceros than a horse. It is apparent, and scientifically unfortunate, that the so-called "dawn horse," on which the entire family tree of horses is based, is not a horse at all."*

It is obvious that the horse did not evolve, but it appeared in the fossil record in the same form as it is today.

The Split Hoof Mammals

The split hoofed, or cloven hoof, mammals are classified in the Artiodactyls Order (see Figure 6-2). This group is subdivided into the pig, hippopotamus, camel, deer, giraffe, and the cattle families. Pigs first appeared in the Oligocene, whereas the hippopotamus did not appear until the Pliocene Epoch. Camels first appeared in the Eocene, and were a New World family, which means that **North America was the home of the original camel** to the end of the Pleistocene Epoch. See Figure 6-5. These early camels mysteriously disappeared at the time of the great extinctions that took place at the sudden termination of the Pleistocene Epoch. Why did they suddenly disappear? This will be explained in the sequel Volume Two to this manuscript by H. Donald Daae.[14] Today modern camels are only found in Old World countries such as North Africa, the Middle East and parts of Southeast Asia. An exception is the llamas, which are classified with the camel family, and are found in South America.

The deer family first appeared in Miocene time. They include the caribou, elk, moose, and wapiti, among others.

Cattle: Cattle are considered one of the "Beasts of the Earth" in the Bible (Deuteronomy 14:4). They are land animals, having all the characteristics of other warm blooded mammals. The buffalo, wild sheep, and wild goats are also classified with the cattle family, and first appeared in Europe and Asia in Late Miocene time.

Biblical scholars have often questioned why cattle should be singled out from other beasts in the Genesis record. There are two possible explanations. First, cattle represent a "clean" animal that is used for man's food consumption. A list of the clean animals is given as follows in Deuteronomy 14:4-8 (NIV), *"⁴These are the animals you may eat: the ox, the sheep, the goat,⁵the deer, the gazelle, the roe deer, the wild goat, the ibex, the antelope and the mountain sheep.⁶You may eat any animal that has a divided hoof and that chews the cud. ⁷However, of those that chew the cud or that have a divided hoof you may not eat the camel, the rabbit or the hyrax. Although they chew the cud, they do not have a divided hoof; they are ceremonially unclean for you. ⁸The pig is also unclean; although it has a divided hoof, it does not chew the cud. You are not to eat their meat or touch their carcasses."*

The people of Israel were instructed to eat animals with a split hoof divided in two and that chewed the cud. If an animal did not have both of these characteristics then it was not to be eaten. These instructions were given to the Israelites for health reasons.

Throughout the ages cattle have been domesticated by man. It is the animal most commonly used by man for meat. Since the beginning of civilization, the well-being of man has been closely linked with the domestication of cattle, goats and sheep.

Secondly, cattle have been singled out because of their role as "clean animals" for sacrifice. The shedding of blood is a vital part of God's plan for the redemption of mankind in the Old Testament from the time of Adam and Eve to the Cross. Prior to the Cross, the shed blood of clean animals has served as a covering and cleansing of man's sins. In the Old Testament it is recorded in Leviticus 17:11, NKJV, *"For the life of the flesh is in the blood; and I have given it to you upon the altar to make an atonement for your souls, for it is the blood that makes an atonement for your soul."*

When the Creator, Jesus Christ was crucified on the Cross, He shed his sinless blood for the sins of the world. From that time onward all animal sacrifices ceased.

In the New Testament it is recorded: *"And almost all things are by the law purged with blood; and without the shedding of blood there is no forgiveness"* (Hebrews 9:22). We read in 1 John 1:7, *"If we walk in the light, as he is in the light, we have fellowship one with another and the blood of Jesus Christ his Son cleanses us from all sin."* If a person is willing to admit his sins and is willing to confess his sins and is willing to also receive Jesus Christ into his or her heart then we read in 1 John 1:9 NKJV, *"He is faithful and just to forgive your sins and to cleanse you from all unrighteousness."*

The 35 or so Phyla

All warm blooded mammals are chordates in that they have a vertebral column with a notochord within. **They all relate to the Chordate Phyla (Body Plan)** that were established during the Lower Cambrian Explosion of Animal Life. However, during the Lower Cambrian there were also 34 or more other body plans called phyla that have continued to the present day.

It is possible that this particular category, called "Creeping Things" would be representative of all of the other 34 or so phyla (body plans) that have continued to survive to the present day. Today, there are multi invertebrate species and other multi species of germs, micro organisms and bacteria, etc. that would also relate to each of these 34 or so other body plans. See Figures 1-12 & 1-1.

Invertebrate Life

The multi Phyla represented by invertebrate life fit neatly into the Creeping Things category. Raymond C. Moore[15] said, *"The invertebrate life of the Cenozoic era is rich and varied. Thousands of fossil species have been collected and described, and each year brings important additions to knowledge of this branch of paleontology. The outstanding characters of the invertebrate fauna as a whole are the progressively increased resemblance to the living fauna, the dominance of pelecypods and gastropods, and the common very perfect preservation of the shells, which in many cases are hardly altered at all."* Then Moore[14] says, *"Mollusks occupy the dominant place among Cenozoic invertebrates. This is due to the abundance of pelecypods and gastropods, the species of which are numbered by the thousands."* He then continues to describe the protozoans, the echinoderms, the bryozoans, the brachiopods, sponges and corals.

I admire the invertebrate paleontologists who are able to determine the specific age of each geological Epoch by the continual new and uniquely different invertebrate fossil species and assemblages of fossils that appear. These species identify whether an oil company is drilling in sediments of the Paleocene, Eocene, Oligocene, Miocene, Pleistocene or Recent Epochs. In other words, these assemblages of invertebrate animal life are present worldwide wherever drilling takes place. See Figure 1-1.

Within exploration companies who are exploring for oil and gas, the idea of evolution or creation is never discussed. It is only the elite group of Professors in our universities who widely discuss the idea of evolution and the origin of the species. It is here where a Professor dares not even mention the possibility of any fossil ever being created by an Almighty Creator God. No one is allowed to imply at our universities that these species may have ever been intelligently designed.

The Darwinists have gained control of our educational institutions. Their premise is that every species has evolved by a naturalistic, unintelligent evolutionary process. Up to the present time, these Darwinian Professors are still trying to find the true answers. There are many theories, but they do not adequately or even come close to explaining how a certain species can possibly evolve into another distinct and unique species. It is only a matter of time before the Darwinists will begin to acknowledge the weakness of their position.

The Pleistocene Epoch

Let us now briefly recap the generally warm climate that prevailed throughout the Mesozoic Era (the Fifth Day). This warm climate continued throughout most of the Cenozoic Era (the Sixth Day) to the end of the Pliocene Epoch. See Figure 1-1.

It was during the latter part of the Pliocene Epoch when the first indications of cooler weather in the form of ice first appeared. This cooler weather intensified at the beginning of the Pleistocene Epoch when a fully fledged Ice Age commenced. See Figures 1-1.

According to the science of geology, **the Pleistocene Epoch began about 2.5 million years ago and ended about 4500 years ago.** It was at this time that the Recent Age was ushered in. See Figure 6-5.

It is interesting to observe that the Pleistocene Ice Age is the last of five major Ice Ages that have been geologically identified throughout the entire geological history of the Earth. See Figure 1-1. They are as follows:

1. The Lower Proterozoic Gowganda Ice Age (Glaciation).
2. The Upper Proterozoic Ice Age (Glaciation).

3. The Upper Ordovician Ice Age (Glaciation).
4. The Lower Permian Ice Age (Glaciation).
5. **The Pleistocene Ice Age (Glaciation).**

All of these above mentioned major Ice Ages or Glaciations have left an indelible imprint within the geological history of the Earth. However, the long in-between geological ages have been mild and free of ice.

My personal belief is that God allowed these periods of glaciations to cleanse and to revitalize the Earth's environment in preparation for new developments and new creations of plant and animal life.

The term Pleistocene was first defined by Charles Lyell in 1833 from a Quaternary aged succession of sediments in Sicily. Clark and Stern[17] quote Charles Lyell who said, *"The criterion for separating the Pleistocene beds from the underlying Pliocene beds was the greater similarity of the fauna of the upper beds with modern fauna."* In other words, the many animal fauna like the now extinct woolly mammoth, the mastodon and saber tooth tiger, giant sloth, giant beaver, a three toed horse and many more all characterize the Pleistocene Ice Age. These animals were some of the many inhabitants of the Earth during this long period of time. However, what actually happened to these strange Pleistocene animals? Why did they become extinct? Figure 6-4 is an artist's rendition of what a woolly mammoth looked like.

Some persons scoff at the idea that the Pleistocene Ice Age (Glaciation) could possibly have been a long period of time that could have extended into the past for about 2.5 millions of years. I have had the privilege of analyzing some of these Pleistocene sediments and have come to realize that the Pleistocene Epoch was indeed a long period of time.

I was privileged to have been employed with a certain major oil and gas company who participated in the drilling of a Joint Company COST well in the offshore Gulf of Alaska region. This well was drilled to about 13,000 feet (3960 m) below sea bottom. It encountered over 4,000 feet (1220 m) of sediment of Pleistocene Age. This was determined by our company's consulting paleontologists who were able to identify the invertebrate animal fossil life that belonged exclusively to the Pleistocene age. Seismic data revealed that these sediments were continuing to increase in thickness in a southern seaward direction.

I was also involved with another major company who were assessing the hydrocarbon potential within the Mackenzie Delta region of Northern Canada. The Pleistocene sediments in the vicinity of the Inuit communities of Aklavik and Inuvik are relatively thin. On the basis of seismic, one could trace the gradual thickening of the Pleistocene sediments in a northern direction to where they were locally considered to be in the vicinity of about 7,500 feet (2280 m) in thickness in the more localized offshore Mackenzie Delta region of the Beaufort Sea. This great thickness of sediments reveals to us that it would have taken a considerable period of time for these Pleistocene sediments to have been deposited.

The Pleistocene Epoch is estimated by geologists to cover a time span of about 2.5 million years. This is based upon radiometric methods of dating. This age can be subdivided into four colder glacial advance periods referred to in North America as the Nebraskan, Kansan, Illinois and Wisconsin glaciations with three intervening warmer periods referred to as the Aftonian, Yarmouth and the Sangamon as shown on Figure 6-5. The Wisconsin Glacial advance was the most extensive advance of glacial ice. This was followed by an exceptionally warm and moist period called the Post Wisconsin Age when the ice edge retreated a significant distance. In the Old World of Europe and Asia, these subdivisions have different names, but what took place in northern Europe and Asia parallels what took place in North America.

The different transgressive and regressive stages of the Pleistocene Ice Age have revealed that the main core of glacial ice remained in place. The thickness of the ice has been estimated to have been in excess of 15,000 feet (3,048 m) in thickness in the central core regions. In other words, the shaded regions in Figure 6-5 remained covered by ice throughout the Pleistocene except along the southern margins. In Europe and Asia and in North America, the southern edges of glacial ice have been well documented by various geological studies.

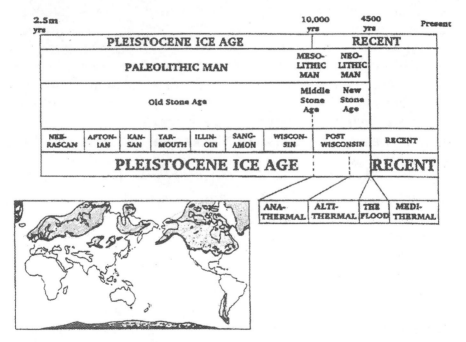

Figure 6-5: This Figure reveals how Darwinists relate Early Man to the entire Pleistocene Ice Age. The above map reveals the areas of the Earth that were covered by ice during this Pleistocene Ice Age. The Recent Age relates to Modern Man. Prepared by Don Daae.

The glacial deposits throughout the southern portions of Canada consists of a mixtures of boulder clay mixed with rock boulders and pockets or lenses of sand or gravel. The rock boulders, large and small, were brought down from the more northerly Precambrian Shield regions. As the glacial ice moved southward, it brought large and small granite and other crystalline Archean rocks southward and deposited them with a mixture of reworked younger clay and sandstone rocks that are commonly referred to as boulder clay. This glacial boulder till is present throughout the more southerly portions of the prairie provinces of Alberta, Saskatchewan and Manitoba in Western Canada. This boulder clay averages about 200 feet (60 m) in thickness. Some places it is thinner and other places it increases to over 900 feet (270 m). This in itself suggests that considerable time was involved in the deposition of the glacial till. There are also pockets of sand and gravel within the till. The water in these sand pockets is generally alkaline and not too suitable for drinking.

It is believed that the maximum advance of the ice development was achieved during the Wisconsin Age. Then, about 10,000 years before the present, the climate throughout the Earth entered into an exceptional period of pronounced warming called the Post Wisconsin Age. This age can also be divided more accurately into the Anathermal and the Altithermal Ages as shown on Figure 6-5.

My Early Perception of the Ice Age

I was raised on a farm in southeastern Saskatchewan about 10 miles north of the USA boundary of North Dakota and about 25 miles west of the town of Estevan. My Dad's farm was loaded with large and small glacial erratic boulders. My big question at that time was how did these boulders ever get on my Dad's land? They sure gave us a lot of heavy work to do. They consisted primarily of Pre-Cambrian granite and granodiorites as well as many other types of dark crystalline basalt, andesite & volcanic igneous rocks that had been transported by glacial ice from the Great Canadian Shield region in Northern Saskatchewan. My three older brothers and I spent many hours laboriously picking these rocks from the fields and dragging the larger ones by horse or tractor to large stone piles. To my brothers and to me these glacial erratics were a pain.

When I became a young geologist, I began to work for British American Oil Company which later became Gulf Oil Canada. I was transferred to Regina, Saskatchewan. I was then delegated to be the well site geologist on a well that was to be drilled within the Frobisher Oil Field near the town of Estevan. The oil from this Field was producing from two separate zones known as the Midale and the Frobisher Alida Beds within the limestone formation of Mississippian Age.

The wildcat well that I was assigned to was to be a deep 11,000+ foot (3350 +meter) test well that would evaluate all the geological formations from the Pleistocene to the crystalline basement rocks of Archean Age. See Figure 1-1.

During brief in between times, I would visit my brother's farm. I would eventually end up at the old rock piles examining the different rock types. As a result of my university training and my experience with an oil company, I was now able to identify and to describe the various Archean (basement) rock types. However, my big discovery was to find some light grey, fossiliferous limestone boulders of Silurian / Ordovician age. The big question then arose, how did these limestone rocks get onto my Dad's land? I also came to realize that these same aged rocks were also present about 8000+ feet (2400+ meters) below my Dad's farm. I had just drilled through this same sequence of limestone rocks at the well I was attending. I then realized that all of these older formations continued to extend northward and eventually would come to the surface as rock outcrops along the southern edge of the Precambrian Shield region in northern Saskatchewan. The glaciers then carried these fossiliferous rocks southward to my Dad's farm.

Today, I view these old Archean granite crystalline rocks within a different geological perspective. According to the science of geology the Archean Period is believed to have extended from about 3.8 to about 4.6 billion years into the past. This is based upon radiometric dating. I can now imagine this early time in the history of the Earth when God had prepared this most beautiful, magnificent Garden called Eden for the Earth's first inhabitants "Lucifer and his angels." See Figure 1-4. See Chapter One for greater details.

I now realize that the reason why these animal fossils are present in the Silurian/Ordovician limestone boulders is because they had experienced death. This death was a result of the Edenic Curse that fell upon the Earth at the time when Lucifer sinned and after he had chosen to rise up against Almighty God. This tragic event took place at the termination of the Archean Period. See Figure 1-1.

The Post Wisconsin Age

It was during the exceptionally warm Post Wisconsin Age that a NW/SE trending "Ice Corridor" formed in Western Alberta. This narrow Ice Corridor extended northward into the northern Yukon Territories and westward through Central Alaska and westward into Russia. It then became a migratory pathway for Early Man to enter into North and South America from Asia.

This new age from 10,000 years to about 4,500 years before the present is often classified as the geological Post-Wisconsin Age. It can also be subdivided into the Anathermal and the Altithermal ages as shown in Figure 6-5. All of the now extinct Pleistocene animals such as the mastodon, the woolly mammoth, the saber tooth tiger, the giant sloth and so forth were all present throughout the

Earth in great numbers to the end of the Post-Wisconsin Age. What happened to them? Why are they not present with us today?

Based upon the science of geology, the Pleistocene Age mysteriously came to a sudden termination. This extraordinary event brought the Post-Wisconsin Age to a sudden end.

There is another perplexing problem and that is how does Early Man relate to the Pleistocene Ice Age? See Figure 6-5. Is it possible to relate Early Man to the entire Pleistocene Ice Age as Darwinists attempt to do?

Who Was Early Man?

A mystery surrounds the origin of Early Man. He was the one who occupied the so called Old World consisting of Europe, Asia, Africa and Australia and also the New World which was North and South America during the Pleistocene Ice Age. Where did Early Man come from? What did he look like? What kind of tools did he have? Was he a Stone Age Man? Was he intelligent? What were his accomplishments?

There were only two basic types of Early Man. They were the Neanderthal Man and the Cro-Magnon Man. The Neanderthal Man primarily occupied China, Mongolia, Australia, North & South America whereas the Cro-Magnon Man primarily occupied Europe, Western Asia, the Middle East, Egypt / Africa. These questions are often asked: What were their phenomenal accomplishments? What happened to the Neanderthal Man and why did he become extinct?

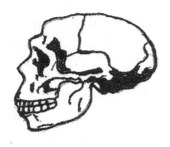 

The Neanderthal Man   The Cro-Magnon Man

Figure 6-6: Illustrates the facial features of the two types of Early Man. They are the Neanderthal and the Cro-Magnon Man. Drawn and prepared by Don Daae after MacGowan & Hester, p.89.[18]

This Early Man lived coincident with the pre-historic animals such as the now extinct giant elephants like the mastodon, the woolly mammoth, the saber tooth tiger, extinct bison, giant sloths, apes called Hominids and the list could go on and on. Some of these now extinct animals were definitely present on Earth for up to 2.5 million years into the past. The big question arises, how far back in time is it possible to trace Early Man?

Darwinian paleo-anthropologists and paleo-archaeologists view Early Man in an evolutionary framework. It is claimed that Early Man has descended from certain primitive apes, or ape-like, ancestors called hominids that go back in time for several millions of years.

Darwinian anthropologists maintain that the Cro-Magnon man evolved from the Neanderthal man who in turn evolved from certain ape like creatures such as Homo erectus, Homo habilis and down the chain to Australopithecus afarensis (Lucy) and to Ardipithecus ramidus called Ardi.

Lucy is now classified as Australopithecus afarensis and is believed to have lived about 3.7 million years into the past, whereas, Ardi who is classified as Ardipithecus ramidus is believed to have lived about 4.4 million years ago. What is the reasoning behind this mysterious evolutionary linked chain?

The Primates and Early Man

The primates deserve special attention, because Darwinists always relate Early Man to the primates. In fact, man is classified as a true primate, having similar characteristics with other primates such as the prosimians, the monkeys and the apes.

The Bible says that man and woman are unique and different from other members of the animal world because they were created in the image of God. No other species of animal life was ever created in the image of God.

The question arises as to who were Homo erectus and Homo habilis? It is believed that they lived during the Pleistocene Ice age. This was during the last 2.5 million years of Earth's history. Are they related to Early Man? Another intriguing question is this: How is Early Man related to Modern Man?

In order to resolve this issue, I encourage our reader to read a detailed account of the Primates and Early Man in H. Donald Daae's[19] book, "Bridging the Gap: The 7th Day, Who Was Early Man – Vol. 2, Age of Phenomenal Accomplishments." The big questions that will be answered are: when did True Man called Homo sapiens first appear on Earth and what were his phenomenal accomplishments? It will also answer the question as to his appearance and the kind of tools he had developed. It will answer the many other questions regarding Early Man's ancestry.

Conclusion

Today as we look back in time, we realize that Early Man lived contemporary with the many species of Pleistocene animal life like the saber toothed tiger, the woolly mammoth, the mastodon and many other pre-historic animals that were present in great numbers throughout the Earth during the Pleistocene Epoch. Why did they suddenly disappear? What happened to them? Another big question is this: what happened to the thousands of feet (meters) of massive sheets of ice that still covered large portions of Canada and northern Europe and Asia at this point in time? See Figure 6-5.

The geological, archaeological, anthropological and Biblical details surrounding the origin and history of Early Man and Woman are beyond the scope of this manuscript.

Man and Woman were God's final and crowning acts of Creation. The moment Adam and Eve sinned, the Sixth Day came to an abrupt end and the Seventh Day began. If we would advance no further with our study of the history of the Earth, we would fail to resolve many issues that surround the current debate regarding Early Man's ancestry, his descendants and his phenomenal accomplishments.

Afterword

As we have progressed step-by-step, systematically examining the geological history of the Earth in light of Biblical evidence, the great and small pieces of the puzzle have come together in a most precise and orderly manner. The evidences presented by geology and the related Earth sciences complete the framework and discourse presented by the Bible. It makes one conscious of the scientific accuracy of the Holy Scriptures and how they precisely relate to the science of geology, paleo-archeology and paleo-anthropology. The late Dr. Wernher Von Braun,[20] a leading space scientist, expressed this in 1966 as follows, *"Science and religion are not antagonists, but sisters. Both seek ultimate truth. Science helps to reveal more about the Creator through his creation."*

References for the 6th Day

1. Simon Conway Morris "The Crucible of Creation," Oxford University Press, Oxford, New York, Melbourne, p.169.
2. Carl 0. Dunbar and Karl M. Waage, *Historical Geology*, Third Edition (New York: John Wiley and Sons, Inc., 1969, p.272. Emphasis added. P.448
3. Google: the K/T Boundary.
4. A. Lee McAllister, The History of Life, Foundations of the Earth Science Series (London and Toronto, Prentice-Hill International, Inc, 1962), p.122.
5. A. Lee McAllister, p.126.
6. Clark & Stearne, "Geological Evolution of North America," Second Edition, 1968, The Ronald Press Company, USA, p. 498.
7. Clark & Stearne p. 498-499.
8. Clark & Stearne. 498.
9. Dunbar & Waage. p. 461.
10. Dunbar & Waage. p. 479.
11. Dunbar & Waage. P. 464.
12. Duane Gish, "The Challenge of the Fossil Record." El Cajon, Calif., Creation Life Publishers, n.d.), p.82.
13. Duane Gish, p. 82.
14. H. Donald Daae, "Bridging the Gap The 7th Day Who Was Early Man – Vol. 2, Age of Phenomenal Accomplishments. 2010, WestBow Press, Bloomington, Indiana. Chapters 7 & 8. See www. gira.ca.
15. Raymond C. Moore, "Historical Geology," McGraw-Hill Book Company, Inc., New York & London, 1933, p.623.-627.
16. Raymond C. Moore, p.623.
17. Clarke & Stearne, p. 380.
18. MacGowan Kenneth & Hester Joseph A., "Early Man in the New World," published in co-operation with the American Museum of Natural history. The

Natural History Library Anchor books, Doubleday & Company, Inc. Garden City, N.Y. 1962, p.89.
19. H. Donald Daae, aa. Chapters 8-30.
20. Dr. Wernher Von Braun, The Farther We Probe into Space, The Greater My Faith, Springfield, MO.: Assemblies of God," 1966.

APPENDIX A

The Biblical God of Creation

The God of the Bible is all powerful (omnipotent), everywhere present (omnipresent), and all knowing (omniscient). He has always been and always will be. He is the God of the universe and is portrayed as a three-in-one relationship, one God with three distinct personalities: God the Father, God the Son, and God the Holy Spirit. In relation to the physical universe, God the Father can be likened to the "Master Architect," God the Son to the "Master Creator," and God the Holy Spirit to the "Infinite Indweller." See Figure 1-3.

It was in the beginning that God the Father, the great Master Architect came forth with an architectural blueprint or plan for the entire universe. Within God the Father is found all the power to create. He could have created each individual sphere in space, but he chose to assign the actual work of creation to God the Son, the Great Divine Creator and Contractor of the universe, who carried out the perfect will and plan of God the Father by creating, forming and making the heavens and the Earth. We are told that, *"All things were made by Him and without Him was not anything made that was made"* (John 1:3). The Holy Spirit was sent to indwell, to fill, and to perpetuate this vast area of creation. God the Holy Spirit has the inherent power to create. He could have created the universe, but He didn't, because the work of creation was delegated to God the Son.

It is important to keep in mind that God the Father, God the Son and God the Holy Spirit cooperated in the overall work of planning, designing, creating, forming and maintaining the universe. To illustrate, an architect is involved in the work of planning large buildings. The contractor is involved with the work of construction, and the people who occupy the building are the indwellers. Thus, we begin to see that all three persons of the Godhead were involved in the overall work of creation, but each had a different unique role to play.

The very first verse of Genesis brings out the plurality of the Godhead in creation as follows: "*In the beginning God created the heavens and the earth.*" (Gen. 1:1) The Hebrew word for God in this verse is ELOHIM, which has the Hebrew ending most commonly used for masculine nouns in the plural. A devout Hebrew scholar of two centuries ago, Dr. Parkhurst[1] defined the word *Elohim* as a name usually given in the scriptures to the Trinity by which they represent themselves as under the obligation of an oath. According to this definition the *Elohim* covenanted not only with the creation but, as the Godhead, within itself. See Figure 1-3.

Creation is the act of the *Elohim.* In Colossians we see that Christ, the second person of the Godhead is within the *Elohim* as follows: "*For in Him were ALL THINGS CREATED, that are in heaven, and that are in earth, visible and invisible—all things were CREATED by him, and for him.*" (Colossians 1:16) and again we read as follows: "All things were MADE by him, and without him was not anything made that was made" (John 1:3).

Then in Genesis we read that the Spirit of *Elohim* moved or brooded over the waters as follows: "*And the Spirit of God moved upon the face of the waters*" (Gen. 1:3). This is the first mention of God the Holy Spirit who is involved with the perpetuation and the indwelling of all creation.

According to Nathan Stone,[2] *Elohim* is always in the plural form, but is accompanied by verbs and adjectives in the singular. In the first verse of Genesis the verb "create" is singular as it is throughout the Bible. In many places we find singular pronouns, such as "I am *Elohim* and there is no *Elohim* beside me" (Isaiah 15:5, NIV). *Elohim* often speaks of himself as "us" or "our": *"Let us make man in our image, in our likeness"* (Genesis 1:26) NIV; and also when God came down to earth and dispersed the nation of Babel throughout the earth God said, *"Let us go down and confuse their language"* (Genesis 11:7, NIV). A third example is when the prophet Isaiah was given a glimpse of the Lord of heaven and Earth high and lifted up sitting upon a throne. God said to the prophet, "Whom shall I send, and who will go for us." (Isaiah 6:8. NIV). In both the Old and New Testaments the Trinity of the Godhead is revealed through the word *Elohim* as a plurality: the Father, the Son, and the Holy Spirit.

According to Stone,[3] the Hebrew word *Elohim* also expresses the idea of greatness and glory, including creative and governing power, omnipotence, and sovereignty. From Genesis 1:1 to 2:4 the only word used for 'God' is *Elohim,* which appears thirty five times. It is *Elohim* who by his mighty power creates the universe by the power of his word and the breath of his mouth. In other words, he is the possessor and ruler of all heaven and Earth, whose presence cannot be confined by space or time. The Bible says that he fills all space which is recorded, *"Do not I fill all heaven and earth says the Lord"* (Jeremiah 23:24).

God has a plan for the universe which has been in operation for multi-millions of years. It is going on at present and will continue into the future into all ETERNITY!

References

1. Parkhurst, Hebrew Lexicon, see Elohim.
2. Stone, Nathan J., "Names of God" (Chicago: The Moody Press, 1944).
3. Stone, ibid.

APPENDIX B

Yom: The Earth's Long Days

The Bible reveals that God created the Earth in six days *(yomim)* and rested on the Seventh Day (yom). The question arises, when did the First Day begin and when did the Sixth Day end? Are we living in the Seventh Day today? Did the First Day begin about 6000+ years ago as some contend, or did it begin millions of years ago? How long could each of these days have been? Were they seven 24-hour days, or is it possible that they were long periods of time, perhaps millions of years in duration?

According to the Bible, the First Day of Creation began the moment God began his work of old (Proverbs 8:22). In other words, the moment that God began to create the very first atom in the physical universe marks the beginning of the First Day of Creation.

The Hebrew word *yom* means day and has the following three basic meanings:

- a 24-Hour day
- a period of time
- a period of daylight

Yom occurs over 1480 times in the Old Testament and can be rendered in English translation by 50 different words, such as "life," and "forever," in addition to words like "day" or "time." In the New Testament the equivalent Greek words *Semera* and *Hemera* are also used many times, and sometimes refer to an event. For example, "The DAY of the Lord will come as a thief in the night" (II Peter 3:10). In another reference, "day" is referred to as 1000 years (II Peter 3:8), indicating God's timelessness and the fact that his "day" is not confined to Earth days.

The first chapter of Genesis is called the CREATION WEEK, and contains the first mention of the word "day" *(yom).* This is a key to its meaning elsewhere in the Bible, and offers a clue as to whether *yom* has a flexible or an inflexible meaning. Theologians refer to the *Law of First Mention* as a valuable aid in Bible study. It is generally stated like this: "The first time a phrase, word, event or incident occurs in the Bible, it gives a key to its meaning elsewhere in the Bible."

The first mention of the word "day" is found in Genesis 1:5, *"And God called the light DAY, and the darkness he called NIGHT."* This means that the sun was shining upon the newly created Earth with darkness on one side and light on the other, the same as we experience today. See Figure 1-2. Accordingly, the first mention of the word "day" *(yom)* refers to a period of daylight, which is a variable period of time. For instance, the amount of sustained daylight varies dramatically from place to place depending on the season of the year and the latitude of the location. Towards the polar regions of the Earth, for example, one experiences 4 to 5 months of continuous daylight in summer, and only a matter of minutes in winter. This variability gives the word "day" a metaphorical aspect. However, from God's perspective, the Creation days could be millions of earth years in duration.

The second mention of the word "day" *(yom)* is found in Genesis 1:5b, *"And the evening and the morning were the First Day."* Many scholars believe that this phrase refers to a 24-hour period of time. It is held here that this refers more abstractly to a time of planning and a time of working. A further example is given in Genesis 2:4, "*These are the generations of the heavens and the earth when they were created, in the DAY (yom) that the Lord God made the earth and the heavens.*" In the context of Genesis 2:4-7 we see that the entire six days of creation are summarized by the word "day." Here the use of the word "day" clearly has a metaphorical aspect, abstractly referring to a period of time, rather than a period of daylight or a 24-hour time period.

There are many other references to show that the word *yom* or "day" refers simply to a non-specific period of time. Job 18:20 states, "*They that come after him shall be astonished at his day.*" Here "day" refers to the entire lifespan of Job, or to the time that he was going through all his trouble. Psalm 137:7 tells about "*In the Day of Jerusalem.*" Here the word "day" refers to the entire 70 year period that Jerusalem was held in captivity by Babylon.

Some theologians hold that Exodus 20 indicates that the "Creation Week" was comprised of seven 24-hour day periods, thus placing the beginning of the first day of creation at about 6000+ years ago. God had just given the Ten Commandments to Moses. In the 7th Commandment, the Lord confirms the "work week" with the nation of Israel as follows: "*Remember the Sabbath day (yom) to keep it holy. Six days (yomim) shall you labor, and do all your work. But the 7th day (yom) is the Sabbath of the Lord thy God.*" (Exodus 20:8-10). In this context it is evident that each "day" of the "work week" refers to a 24-hour time period. Then the Lord compares the "Work Week" with the "Creation Week" as follows: "*For in six days (yomim) the Lord made heaven and earth, the sea, and all that in them is, and rested the seventh day (yom) wherefore the Lord blessed the Sabbath Day, and hallowed it*" (Exodus 20:11). On the basis of the Law of First Mention, however, the word *yom* in Genesis 1:5 (in the context of the "Creation Week") refers to a non specific period of daylight, or to a duration of time of variable length. This implies that each of the seven days can be expected to be of varying duration. There is no real justification for assuming that the seven *yomin of* the work week are the same length as the seven *yomin* of the creation week. A 24-hour day is only one of the several meanings that can be applied to the Hebrew word *yom.* This is borne out when scripture is compared with scripture.

Hebrews Chapter Four implies that the seventh day *(yom)* equates to several thousand years. It began the moment Adam and Eve sinned, and it has continued to the present. This leads one to conclude that if the Seventh Day represents a long period of time, it is equally logical to assume that the other Six Days are also long intervals of time.

The idea of "day" representing a variable period of time is the basis of the **Day Age** concept of creation, which considers each "day" to have been a long, and variable, period of time. Furthermore, each "day" of creation can be linked to specific periods in the geological history of the Earth. See Figure 1-1.

APPENDIX C

The Evening and the Morning

Each of the six days of the "Creation Week" concludes with the unusual phrase, *"The Evening and The Morning."* What does this mean? The Creation Science persons who believe that the Earth was created in six literal 24 hour days believe that this phrase refers to six phases of a 24-hour day.

An alternative concept is that the evening represents the planning stage for each "day," whereas the morning refers to the commencement of the working stage.

In the Middle East it is customary for the day to begin in the evening at sunset and thus the evening was a time of planning in preparation for the work to be done in the morning. The night was a time of rest. The work necessary to carry out the plan conceived the evening before would commence in the morning. Then the work would continue throughout the day until the plan was completed. In the same manner, the Great Divine Architect of the universe, God the Father, formulated a plan during the evening of each day. He then assigned the carrying out of this plan to the Great Creator and Engineer of the universe, God the Son, who went to work in the morning of each day to create, form and make everything according to the plan conceived the previous evening. The creative work continued throughout the Creation Day.

As we analyze the Six Days of Creation we find that each day represents a long period of time. Each day can be divided into a PLANNING STAGE and a WORKING STAGE, or in other words into an EVENING and a MORNING.

We also see that each Creation Day not only tells about the work done, but also reveals the plan that was conceived in the mind of God the Father, the Great Divine Architect. We begin to see the great amount of intelligent thought and mental energy that was invested into each day of creation. Detailed geological and scientific research and development has begun to unravel the intricacies of the world about us. We are beginning to appreciate that there is a profound intelligence operating "behind the scenes," giving instruction, guidance, and direction to all creation.

In like manner, whatever man designs, creates, and makes involves thought. The more complex is the invention, the greater is the mental energy necessary to bring about its completion. For example, a modern electronic computer involves more thought to design and complete than a bow and arrow. This same principle also applies to the creation of the universe. A far greater amount of thought, mental energy, and work was necessary to create the entire physical universe than, say, to create a single atom.

APPENDIX D

Words For God's Creative Acts

Interpretive controversy surrounds the four Hebrew words *kun, bara, yatsar* and *asah* as they pertain to the Six Days of Creation. Some believe that *bara* (to create), *yatsar* (to form) and *asah* (to make) can be, and have been, used interchangeably by the ancient Hebrews. Others believe that they have distinctly different meanings as they pertain to creation and to the creation process. See Figure 1:15.

It is important to consider the different shades of meaning and different uses of Bible words. Often they can appear to be similar to each other, but yet are quite different—such as is found in Isaiah 45:18, "*For thus saith the Lord that created (bara) the heavens; God himself that formed (yatsar) the earth, and made (asah) it; He hath established (kun) it, he created (bara) it not in vain, he formed (yatsar) it to be inhabited. I am the Lord and there is none else.*"

When we consider this verse, we see that there are four action verbs that particularly stand out. They are create *(bara),* formed *(yatsar),* made *(asah)* and establish *(kun).*

Aaron Pick[1] describes these words as follows:

> Bara—Boro, **to create**.
> Yatsar—Yotsar, **to form**, shape.

Asah—Osoh, **to make**, do, exercise.
Kun—Koorn, to rise, raise up, establish, **to plan**.

James Strong[2] describes *bara* as a primitive root (absolute), *"to create"; (qualified) "to cut down" (a wood), "select," "feed" (as formative processes); "choose," "create" (creator), "cut down," "dispatch," "do," "make" (fat). Robert Young describes bara as to "prepare," "form," "fashion," "create."* Alexander Cruden[3] describes *bara* as to *"make out of nothing," to "bring being out of non-entity," and to "change the form, state and situation of matter which is totally indisposed for such a change, and requires as great power as to make out of nothing."*

James Strong[4] describes *yatsar* as a primitive root: "to press, i.e. be narrow"

(through the squeezing into shape); to "mould into a form, especially as a potter"; "figure to determine" (i.e., form a resolution); also "earthen," "fashion," "form," "frame," "make," "maker," "potter," "purpose." *Yatsar means* to "form," "fashion," "frame," "constitute."

James Strong[5] describes *asah* as a primitive root: to "do" or "make," in the broadest sense and widest application (as follows): "accomplish," "advance," "appoint," "apt," "be at," "become," "bear," "bestow," "bring forth," "bruise," "be busy." Robert Young[6] describes asah as "to do," *"make,"* and "to be made." Alexander Cruden describes *asah* as "to create," "frame," or "fashion," "to choose," or "bring that to be which was not so before," to "call one to a new vocation, and fit and qualify him for the same," to "ordain and appoint," to "turn," to "build," to "change one thing."

James Strong[6] describes the Hebrew word *kuwn, koon,* or *kun* as a primitive root; "proper to be erect" (i.e. stand perpendicular); hence (causative) "to set up, in a great variety of applications, whether literally (establish, fix, prepare, apply), or figuratively (appoint, render pure, prosper)": or "certainty," "confirm," "direct," "faithfulness," "fashion," "fasten," "firm," "be fitted," "be fixed," "make preparation," "prepare" (self), "provide," "make provision," (be, make) "ready," "right," "set" (alright, fast, forth), "be stable," "establish," "stand," "tarry," and "established." Robert Young describes *kun* as to "form," "prepare," "establish." Alexander Cruden[7] describes *kun* as to "establish."

Kun

Alexander Cruden[7] describes *kun* as to "establish." The Hebrew verb "establish" used in Isaiah 45:18 comes from the Hebrew root word *kun,* which also has the meaning to prepare and to plan. We read in Proverbs 3:19, *"The Lord by wisdom founded the earth; By understanding He established the heavens"* And in Jeremiah 10:12 we read, *"He made the earth by his power; He has established the world by His wisdom."*

Filby[8] has this to say, *"In the force of the verb kun, then, as used in the Old Testament it clearly means to make something ready beforehand, with a purpose in view, i.e. to prepare, and to do it so completely that no subsequent alterations are necessary, i.e. to stabilize or establish."* Thus, as Jeremiah 10:12 says, *"It requires power to make something, but it requires wisdom to prepare it perfectly for some preconceived task."*

Kun means to make something ready beforehand with a purpose or plan in mind. The plan and purpose for the universe was conceived in the mind of God before it was created. This plan required wisdom. This concept is brought forward in Proverbs 8:22-23 which says, *"The Lord possessed me (wisdom) at the beginning of His way, before His works of old. I have been established from everlasting, from the beginning, before there was ever an earth."*

Bara, Yatsar, and Asah

It has long been argued that these three Hebrew words for God's creative acts are interchangeable because they are sometimes used in successive verses with what appears to be identical meanings. For example, it is written in Genesis 1:26, "Then God said, Let us make *(asah)* man in our image after our likeness . . . ," whereas in verse 27 it says, "So God created *(bara)* man in His own image, in the image of God He created him." On the surface it appears that these two verbs equate.

It is interesting to read from Origen, to whom the original languages of the Bible would have been familiar, points which are referred to by Constance[9] as follows,

"But as Origen and other early commentators noted, by carefully observing what is said and what is not said in these two verses, (Genesis 1:26 & 27), there is an important lesson to be learned, and the lesson hinges upon the difference in meaning between these two governing verbs, asah and bara."

The first mention of *bara* is found in Genesis 1:1, *"In the beginning God created (bara) the heavens and the earth."* The **primary and absolute meaning** of the word *bara* is to create the earth out of nothing, to bring being out of non-entity and to fulfill a certain purpose. Creation is always instantaneous. The Bible says in Psalm 148:56, *"He commanded and they were created."* By the power of His word the Earth was created in a state of perfection. Each atom and particle of matter was brand new, in, as it happened, a hot gaseous state. From that point onward, however, the first and second laws of thermodynamics and entropy began to apply. The Earth began to age. It began to radiate heat and light energy in all directions. It began to cool. It was at this point in time that the Creator would have begun to form *[yatsar]* the Earth and to prepare it for eventual habitation.

Bara

Bara is distinguished from the other Hebrew verbs, *yatsar* and *asah* by being used exclusively with God as the subject. When used as a noun it means the Creator Himself, as we see in Isaiah 40:48, *"The Creator (bara) of the ends of the earth,"* and in Ecclesiastes chapter 12:1 *"Remember now thy Creator (bara) in the days of thy youths."*

While the Hebrew verb *bara* primarily means to create out of nothing (or out of no previous existing material), it does not necessarily only imply creation from nothing. A secondary meaning is given by Alexander Cruden[10] when he says, *"Bara is to change the form, state and situation of matter, which is totally indisposed for such a change, and requires as great power as to make out of nothing."* For example, when God created man in adult form, He first formed man's body out of the dust of the ground (Genesis 2:7), then He breathed into man's body the breath of life, and man became a living soul. In this miraculous, supernatural transaction the dead dust particles became living flesh and blood. God used previously existing material to create the body of man, and He created *(bara)* the true life, the soul and spirit, within man out of no previous existing material. This act of creation, spoken by God, was instantaneous; however the process of forming man's body out of dust would have taken time. Eve was created utilizing a rib from the body of Adam. In other words, God genetically related woman to man, so that they would be of the same species, thus capable of reproducing fertile offspring. Genesis 2:22 says, *"Then the rib which the Lord God had taken from man He made into a woman."*

Every species of plant and animal life that has ever lived on the Earth was created individually male and female possibly in a similar manner to that of man. However, only man was created in the image of God.

Yatsar

The first mention of the Hebrew verb *yatsar* is found in Genesis 2:22 as follows:

"And the Lord God formed (yatsar) man of the dust of the ground and breathed into his nostrils the breath of life, and man became a living being. "In this context *yatsar* means to form something out of previous existing material. The implication is that of the Master Potter forming a man's body out of the dust of the ground. "Potter" is one of the meanings of *yatsar* which also means "to form," "fashion," or "frame."

Filby[11] says, *"A potter works quickly and the onlooker is impressed by his wonderful skill, but the work is not instantaneous, it grows—it is a process with various stages—and the clay passes from the formless state to the beautifully-formed condition. It is what in modern scientific terms might be called a disorder to order transformation. But it does not arise by itself. The form or pattern does not originate in the clay, it originates in the mind of the potter."*

Isaiah 45:18 says that God created *(bara)* and formed *(yatsar)* the Earth. The implication is that God created the Earth out of nothing, instantaneously, but from that moment onward he has been forming and molding the Earth into a place suitable for habitation. *Yatsar,* to form, implies a process. The task of forming the Earth takes time to do, and involves a step-by-step procedure.

Yatsar also refers to internal processes of change within an object, such as the process of aging and degradation which results in death. Isaiah 43:7 says that God has created *(bara)* and formed *(yatsar)* man for His glory. From the moment that God created man, He has been in the process of forming or molding man. This process of *yatsar* begins at conception and ends at the grave.

Asah

The first mention of the Hebrew word *asah* is found in Genesis 1:7: We read, *"Thus, God made (asah) the firmament, and divided the waters which were under the firmament from the waters which were above the firmament; and it was so."*

In the context of this verse, God did not create *(bara)* the firmament, but he made *(asah)* the firmament. The firmament, or hydrosphere, was made and formed when the oceans were born during the middle part of the First Day. The reference to *asah* in Genesis 1:7 does not refer to a new creation, but rather to the giving of a new appointment or assignment to the firmament. The new appointment was for the purpose of providing a greenhouse effect upon the Earth, in preparation for the future creation of land plants and animal life. Constance[12] says, *"In the Old Testament where the word asah forms part of a personal name, it is most appropriately rendered by the English word "appointed." Thus we have in II Sam 2:18 the name Ahasel, meaning "God has appointed." In 2 Kings 12:15, "we have the name Ahijah which means "Jah has appointed." In I Chronicles 4:35 we have Asiel, which means "appointed of God."*

Constance also says[13] *"Asah always involves working over something which already exists, and usually with a view to changing its form. Sometimes it has more precisely the idea of appointment in the sense that the making is in the future: a multitude of descendants, for example (Genesis 13:16). And it may have the meaning of appointment in a more abstract sense as when a covenant is made between*

God and Israel (Genesis 9:12). At least within biblical usage it never means the creation of something out of nothing."

Allowing the word asah, then, to bear the sense of appointment rather than assuming that it is a synonym for creation, we may observe in Genesis 1:26 that God appointed for man that he should bear His image and His likeness: but that when the plan was put into effect and man is spoken of as having been created, reference is made only to the image.

Then Constance goes on to quote from Origen as follows, *"Origen noted, rightly, that while God intended that man should bear both his image and His likeness, He created only the image, whereas the likeness was something which was 'appointed,' something to be achieved."*[14]

Asah has the more general meaning of "to make" or "to be made." It is used with a great deal of latitude, though never to indicate an absolute origination. It presupposes the existence of things which are to be manipulated into new forms. It also looks back to a prior creation *(bara)*; and secondly to the process of formation *(yatsar)* which the object under discussion has gone through to a certain point in time. For example, *asah* is the term used in Genesis 2:4, where it states "the Lord God made *(asah)* the heavens and the earth." In effect, one is looking at the "finished" product, which will continue to undergo change. In other contexts, *asah* has additional related meanings, such as "to accomplish," "advance," "appoint," "bestow," "bring *forth,"* "finish," "fulfill," "furnish," "gather," "maintain," "observe," "bring to pass," "perform," "prepare," "provide," "set," "work," "yield," and "use." For example, *asah* appears in Genesis 1:16 where it reads "And He made *[asah]* the sun, moon, and stars." Applying the connotation of "appoint," this can be interpreted to mean that God gave the sun, moon and stars a new appointment during the Fourth Creation Day, although their original creation *(bara)* occurred during the First Day. In the meantime, these objects had been subject to a process of continuous change *(yatsar)*.

References for Appendix D

1. Aaron Pick, *Dictionary of Old Testament Words For English Readers* (Grand Rapids, Mich.: Kregel Publications, 1977). This was originally published as the Bible Students Concordance by Hamilton, Adams & Clay (London, 1845).
2. James Strong, *The Exhaustive Concordance of The Bible together with a Comparative Concordance also brief Dictionaries of the Hebrew and Greek words of the Original, with References to the English Words.* (N.Y.: Abingdon Press, 1890).
3. Alexander Cruden, "Cruden's Unabridged Concordance," Fleming H. Revell Company, 1965.
4. James Strong, Ibid.
5. James Strong, Ibid.
6. James Strong, Ibid.
7. Alexander Cruden, ibid.
8. P.195. Fredrik A. Filby, "Creation Revealed, Fleming H. Revell Company, 1963, p.40.
9. Arthur C. Constance, "Without Form or Void." A study of the Meaning of Genesis 1:2, Brockville, Ontario: Doorway papers, 1970, p.178.
10. Alexander Cruden, ibid.
11. Filby, ibid., p.41.
12. Constance, ibid. 179.
13. Constance, ibid. 180.
14. Constance, ibid. 180.

APPENDIX E

Other Creation Concepts

The Catastrophic Flood Theory

The Catastrophic Flood Theory, strongly advocated by Young Earth Creation Science persons state that the entire universe of stars and galaxies, the Earth and all its life-forms were all created in six literal 24-hour days about six to eight thousand years ago. The fossil record and the tremendous thickness of geological sediment from the Precambrian to the commencement of the Pleistocene Ice Age is seen as a direct result of the hydraulic action of Noah's Flood.

Due to the catastrophic actions of Noah's Flood, the simpler, less motile organism were buried first and are therefore found in the lower layers of sedimentary rocks. The more complex, motile organisms reached higher ground and were buried in the upper rock layers. See Figure 1-1.

Present forms of animals, and those found within the Pleistocene Epoch sediments are direct descendants of the animals that were preserved within Noah's Ark. This implies that the now extinct saber toothed tiger; the woolly mammoth, the giant mastodons and the long list of strange looking Pleistocene warm blooded animals are Post Food. The question they have yet to answer is this: What happened to these great numbers of strange Pleistocene animals? What happened to the great thicknesses of Pleistocene Ice that covered all of Canada and portions of northern United States, Northern Europe and Asia?

Creation Science persons believe Noah's Flood is responsible for depositing the multi thousands of feet (meters) of sediments that are present below Pleistocene glacial sediments. They are saying that the entire Pleistocene Ice Age is Post Flood. See Figure 1-1.

The Flood theory envisages a water vapor canopy which formed around the Earth during the Second Creation Day and persisted through to the time of Noah's Flood. This pristine greenhouse-type of environment was humid, with pleasant uniform temperatures, which gave rise to luxuriant plant growth and allowed animal life to flourish in abundance throughout the Earth.

There are various problems associated with this theory. It fails to explain the great thicknesses of sandstones, siltstones, shales, carbonates, reefs, evaporates and so forth that constitute the geological column from the Proterozoic to the Pleistocene Ice Age. It fails to explain where all the sediment came from to deposit layers many tens of thousands of feet thick throughout the Earth. Another problem is that plants show less complex forms in the lower, older, strata and more complex forms in the upper layers. Yet none of the plants are motile, and therefore cannot reach higher ground. Flood Creationists offer certain explanations, but they are very inadequate.

Geology verifies that the animal life within the sedimentary rocks have been deposited in a systematic, mappable manner throughout the Earth, whereas a Catastrophic Flood would have had the tendency to deposit animal life in a helter-skelter fashion.

The science of geology verifies the systematic and mappable distribution of animal and plant fossil assemblages in the many layers of sediment throughout the world. This cannot be explained by the Young Earth Flood Creationists.

The Flood Theory is further refuted by the fact that fossilized human remains of pre-Flood Man have never been found among the fossilized plants and animals that constitute the geological column from Precambrian to the beginning of the Pleistocene Ice Age. See Figure 1-1.

We now know from geology that there have not been any definite remains of man that can definitely be related to the Pleistocene Epoch until the latter part of the Post Wisconsin Age. See Figure 6-5.

An attempt to interpret the geological history of the Earth as a result of Noah's Flood as Creation Science persons are trying desperately to do is impossible.

The Gap Theory

The Gap Theory is often referred to as the Ruination-Reconstruction or sometimes the Restitution Theory. It envisages two creations. The First Creation took place at the beginning of the Archean Age. See Figure 1-1.

This was the time that God created a perfect Earth. It is described in Genesis 1:1. The time of this Creation was millions of years ago, in line with the beginning of the conventional geological history of the Earth. This perfect Earth is often envisaged as being full of life, light, joy and bliss. Everything took place without disturbance in harmony and holiness. God committed this Earth to Lucifer and his angels to administer.

This first creation came to an abrupt and sudden end when Lucifer and his angels sinned and entered into open rebellion against God. Lucifer became known as Satan and the fallen angels as demons. They came under the judgment of God, which turned the Earth into a dark chaos, waste and void. Genesis 1:1 says, *"And the earth was without form and void."* The Gap Theory people interpret the Hebrew verb *"hayah"* as meaning, "to become." They interpret the Hebrew words *tohu-wa-bohu* as waste and void. Thus, they say the Earth became waste and void, which resulted in a vast time gap in which the organisms now known as fossils were living. This time gap encompasses the entire geological time scale. It lasted for many millions of earth years.

This theory believes that about 6000+ years ago God recreated the Earth in six 24-hour days which is described in Genesis 1:2-31. This was a second act of Special Creation. It was at this time that the Earth was made perfect once again with the creation of new species of animal and plant life. It was at this time that God established the beautiful Garden of Eden. He created Adam and Eve who became the first human occupants of this garden. The man Adam, the second ruler of the Earth, was tempted by Satan. He ate of the forbidden fruit in the Garden of Eden. His sin was then passed on to all of his descendants. As a result of Adam and Eve's sin the Earth has "become" cursed once again.

Sauer[1] says that the Gap Theory has the following problems: The Hebrew word *hayah* is rarely used to denote "become." Psalm 118:22 is used to support their interpretation which says, *"The stone which the builders rejected is become the head of the corner."*

According to Sauer[1], its real meaning is simply "was." He says. *"The earth was waste and void. They consider it scarcely convincing when a rare use of a word like "was" is cited to establish such an important doctrine, which is not clearly taught anywhere else in the Bible, whereas the same word has the other simple meaning of "was" in thousands of passages of Scripture. Rules may not be based on exceptions."* [1]

According to Sauer[2], the Gap Theory people support their interpretation of the Hebrew words *Tohu-wa-Bohu* by only two other passages of scripture, Isaiah 34:11 which says *"And He shall stretch out over it the line of confusion (tohu) and the stones of chaos" (bohu,* R.S.V.); also Jeremiah 4:23-26 which says, "*I beheld the earth, and lo, it was waste and void [tohu-wa-bohu]; and the heavens, they had no light. I beheld, and, lo, there was no man, and all the birds of heaven were fled. The fruitful field was a wilderness, and all the cities thereof were broken down at the presence of the Lord, and before His fierce anger.*" In both cases it has the passive meaning of being made desolate and empty.

However, Sauer[3] points out that these words occasionally have a passive meaning in the sense of being made waste or empty, their basic meaning in most passages is simply "formlessness," "desert," and "emptiness." For example Job 26-7, "*He stretches out the north over the empty space [tohu]."* Isaiah 40:17 says, "*All nations are as nothing [tohu] before Him.*" Isaiah 59:4 says, "*They trust in vanity, emptiness, tohul and speak lies."* Sauer says, "*It is very risky to base such an important interpretation of Scripture or an exceptional and rare use of the words, whose normal meaning is quite different. It is surely more advisable to interpret the words tohu and bohu in their general and usual sense of 'formlessness' and 'emptiness,' i.e. as a simple description of the original form of the earth at the beginning of creation, as the characterization of the lack of content and form of the mass before the beginning of the Divine, creative impulses."*[3]

When analyzing the last 10,000 years of Earth's history, there are no valid geological evidences to indicate that the Earth was in a state of waste and void or ruination prior to 6,000 years ago as the Gap Theory would indicate. There are no supporting verses throughout the Bible to indicate two separate creations.

When the Gap Theory is analyzed it is found to contain gaps which cannot be accounted for by scripture or by science. Attempts to interpret the geological history of the Earth by means of the Gap Theory leave many questions unanswered.

Our Day Age Creation Concept

Don Daae's[4] second book demonstrates on the basis of geology, paleo-archaeology and paleo-anthropology that Noah's Flood was worldwide and that it resulted in the termination of the Pleistocene Epoch. It also resulted in the extinctions of Pre-Flood Man and all Pleistocene animal life except for Noah and his family and all the land animals that were preserved in Noah's Ark. In this book each Biblical Age relates to a certain Geological Age.

References

1. Erich Sauer. *"The King of the Earth," The High Calling of Man According to the Bible* & *Science* (Palm Springs: Haynes Publishers, inc., 1981), p. 235.
2. Sauer, p. 234.
3. Sauer, p. 234.
4. Daae H. Donald, "Bridging the Gap The 7th Day Who Was Early Man—Vol. 2 What Were His Phenomenal Accomplishments?" WestBow Press, a Division of Thomas Nelson, 1663, Liberty Drive, Bloomington, IN 47403, www.westbowpress.com and www.gira.ca.

APPENDIX F

Dating the Universe & the Earth

The age of the universe is believed to be somewhere between 12 to 16 billion years old. This estimate is based upon measurements of the distance between galaxies. The assumption is that our universe is expanding from a primordial centre, with each galaxy believed to be flying outward at fixed speed. However, astronomers today are saying that the age of the universe is more likely to be about 14 billion years old.

To measure the speed and distance of galaxies in outer space, astronomers use what is known as the "red shift," or Doppler Effect. As a galaxy moves away from the Earth its color shifts towards the red end of the spectrum, in the same manner that the sound of a receding train whistle becomes deeper in tone as it moves farther away. Light is basically a train of waves in space. As a lighted object moves away from a viewer, its light waves appear stretched out by the receding motion.

The length of light waves is perceived by our eyes in the form of color. We perceive short waves as blue (an advancing object) and longer waves as red (a receding object). John Wiester[1] says *"In a process called spectrographic analysis, scientists are able to compare the colored spectrum of light from a distant galaxy with the color spectrum from a source that is not moving relative to the Earth. They are then able* to determine the degree of red shift in a receding galaxy's color spectrum and calculate its speed and distance."[1]

Weister[2] says, "The most distant objects that have been observed in space are quasars (quasi-stellar objects) at about 16 billion light years away from the earth. The farthest galaxy that has been observed through our present telescopes is about 6 billion light years away. The vast array of quasars and galaxies are a part of the "visible universe," however whether anything lays beyond these present limits can neither be affirmed or denied."

Astronomers are not in agreement that objects called quasars are being correctly interpreted. They may be simply strange events in the nuclei of galaxies or other unexplained phenomena. If quasars are star-like objects, and their measurements are correct, then the age of the universe can be deduced to be at least 16 billion years old, and the observable galaxies at 6 billion years.

References

1. John L Wiester, *The Genesis Connection* (N.Y.: Thomas Nelson, Inc., 1983), p. 219.
2. Wiester, p. 221.

Methods to Date the Earth

Earth scientists have established the age of the Earth at 4.6 billion years. The oldest earth rocks located in Greenland have radiometric dates of 3.76 billion years, whereas reports from Russia and South Africa indicate ages of about 4 billion years. Moon rocks and meteorites yield ages approaching 4.6 billion years, thus it is assumed that the Earth has shared a common origin and history with the solar system which came into existence about 4.6 billion years ago. According to Weister[1], "sophisticated comparative residual lead isotope analysis from deep sea cores on Earth also indicates an age of 4.6 billion years." It is here conjectured, however, that the Earth is more ancient than this, in keeping with the 14+ billion year age of the universe. Who knows how long the Earth may have been in an extremely hot gaseous, liquid state prior to the time when the Earth had cooled to the place when a solid crystalline crust had begun to form.

1. John L Wiester, *The Genesis Connection* (N.Y.: Thomas Nelson, Inc., 1983), p. 227.

Radioactive Methods of Dating

As soon as Earth's rocks change from a liquid to a crystalline (solid) state, certain built-in radioactive clocks begin to tick. Scientists attempt to estimate the age of the Earth on the basis of these time clocks.

The common methods for dating rocks older than 5 million years are uranium-lead, rubidium-strontium, and potassium-argon. The methods are based on the fact that the elements of U, Rb, and K, often called parent elements, decay radioactively and eventually change to Pb, Sr and Argon respectively. The latter are called daughter elements. The half-life for Uranium-238 is 4,510 million years, for Uranium-235 is 713 million years, for Potassium-40 is 1,300 million years and for Rubidium is 47,000 million years.

The decay rate of a radioactive mineral or rock is usually stated in terms of its half-life. This is the time it takes for half of the atoms of the parent to decay. After the first half-life, there is one-half of the radioactive element that remains, after the second half-life one-quarter is left, then one-eighth is left and it goes on to one-sixteenth, one-thirty-second and so on. Once the rate of decay is known, it is possible to estimate geological age from an uncontaminated sample. This age is determined by finding the ratio between the amount of nuclides that have disintegrated (daughters) and that which has not (parent).

All of the above radiometric age determination methods have margins of error of at least ±5 million years. This margin of error can increase greatly if contamination has taken place. A sample can be dated by these methods provided the following assumptions are true:

1) None of the daughter elements were present in the rocks when it was formed;
2) The rate of decay of the element has remained constant since the time the rock was formed;
3) All the daughter elements in the rock were derived from the parent element that was previously in the rock.

References

1. John L Wiester, *The Genesis Connection* (N.Y.Thomas Nelson, Inc., 1983), p. 219.

Carbon-14 Dating

Radiocarbon dating is a radioactive dating method to date substances up to 50,000 years ago. It is also known as carbon-14 dating, and is used to date fossils such as shells, bones, dead wood and charcoal that contain organic carbon.

Professor Willard F. Libby, who had worked on the Manhattan Project at the University of Chicago in 1949, conceived the basic idea of using radioactive carbon-14 to determine the dates of prehistoric events with greater accuracy.

The method is based on the fact that a radioactive isotope of carbon, carbon-14, is produced by cosmic ray bombardment of the nitrogen atom in the upper atmosphere, and is eventually absorbed by every living thing on the Earth. Since all organisms are continually absorbing and eliminating carbon-14, they all contain roughly the same percentage that is found in the atmosphere and in other living organisms. When the organisms die, they no longer absorb carbon-14 compounds from their environment, and their proportion of carbon-14 begins to diminish as the radioactive atoms disintegrate. After 5570 years the carbon-14 reaches its half-life, which means that at this point there, is only half as much of this radioactive isotope left as there was when the organism died. After 11,140 years, one-quarter remains, after 16,710 years one-eighth remains, after 22,280 years one-sixteenth remains. Beyond this point, the number of remaining carbon-14 isotopes get smaller and smaller and therefore becomes more difficult to measure. After 50,000 years the amount becomes so infinitesimal that its accuracy becomes very suspect. Since the disintegration of radioactive atoms occurs at a known rate, scientists can determine the age of an organic material by measuring its radioactivity, by counting the number of particles omitted by a known amount of material over a given period of time.

The carbon-14 clock appears, at first glance, like the perfect clock for telling how old ancient objects are. However it does have certain limitations some of which are as follows:

1) It is accurate if the incoming solar energy (cosmic ray particles) bombarding our atmosphere has remained constant over the past 50,000 years. Scientists have discovered variations in solar energy by dating ancient wooden samples of known age and by comparing the radiocarbon and tree ring ages of these samples. They have also worked out correction curves in which carbon-14 dates are calibrated with those obtained by dendrologists which go back 3,000 to 4,000 years. Some scientists believe that the marked changes in climate during the Pleistocene Ice Age were due to variation of incoming solar energy which could significantly affect the radiocarbon clock.

2) It is accurate if the level of the ocean has remained constant for the past 50,000 years. Earth sciences have revealed that great fluctuation in sea level have occurred during this time interval. During the Wisconsin Glaciation, the sea level was lower due to water being locked up within large continental ice sheets. A study of modern shorelines reveal terraces several hundred feet above the present sea level. All these changes would impact on the accuracy of the C-14 clock. Two separate offshore shorelines have also been discovered, one at 329 feet (100+ m) and the other at 197 feet (60 m) below sea level. These two shorelines are described in greater detail in Chapter 22 of Volume Two by H. Don Daae.[3]

3) It is accurate if the object has not been contaminated by groundwater, percolating around a wood or bone fragment causing ionic exchange of elements which results in silicification or petrifaction.

4) Carbon-14 dating is subject to natural faults and human error. Mistakes can be made in the way the sample is

taken, packed, labeled, opened or prepared, there is also a chance something can go wrong with the mathematical calculation.

5) The use of coal, oil and other fossil fuels has tremendously increased the amount of ancient carbon in the atmosphere since the beginning of the industrial revolution. This has caused a decrease in the proportion of carbon-14 in the atmosphere and living things. The hydrogen bomb explosions since the 1950s have also increased the amount of carbon-14 and other radioactive debris in the atmosphere. Unfortunately these have not cancelled each other out.[1]

Meanwhile, rain soaking through leaf and root systems of plants that absorb carbon-14 is contaminating the soil and making carbon dating difficult for some time to come. This, however does not affect deeply buried objects.[2]

6) It is suggested by Patterson that long term variations in the intensity of the earth's magnetic field would influence the amount of carbon-14 in the atmosphere and thus would affect the time clock.

It becomes apparent that there are many factors that can prevent an accurate carbon-14 age determination, especially beyond 4000 years ago when changes were more erratic. Thus, carbon-14 dates must be taken with caution when applied to Early Man

References

1. Thomas C. Patterson, *Archeology, the Evolution of Ancient Societies* (N.Y. Prentice-Hall, 1981), p. 15.
2. Philip Van Doren Stern, *Prehistoric Europe From the Stone Age Man to the Early Greeks* (N.Y.: Norton, 1969), p.74.
3. Daae H. Donald, "Bridging the Gap The 7th Day Who Was Early Man—Vol. 2 What Were His Phenomenal

Accomplishments?" WestBow Press, a Division of Thomas Nelson, 1663, Liberty Drive, Bloomington, IN 47403, www.westbowpress.com and www.gira.ca.

Tree Ring Dating

Tree Ring Dating[1], or Dendrochronology, is based on the fact that trees add concentric growth rings each year. When a tree is cut down or a core is taken from it, the age of the tree can be determined by counting the number of growth rings. The width of rings may reflect variations in the weather. When climate conditions are favorable to growth, wider rings are produced, and narrow rings relate to years with less favorable weather conditions. Scientists are able to produce a master chronology by comparing the ring sequences from different trees of overlapping ages. Patterson says *"This technique was first used in the American Southwest, where experts used ponderosa pine trees to construct a calendar that stretched back to 53 B.C. Using the California bristlecone pine, they have developed a master chronology that now extends more than 8000 years into the past."*

References

1. Thomas C. Patterson, *Archeology, the Evolution of Ancient Societies* (N.Y. Prentice-Hall, 1981), p. 14

Varve Method of Dating

Probably one of the most accurate methods of dating the past 10,000 years is based upon the counting of varved, annually laminated, glacial lake clays and silts. Varved clays are formed in fresh water lakes from mud brought by glacial melt water streams. Normally, one light colored, relatively course or silty laminae was deposited in summer, and one dark, greasy laminae in winter. The couplet was called a varve and is frequently about (2 cm) one inch thick. Sequences of varves are measured in clay exposures and the measurements are graphed, correlated and combined in continuous series after a method devised and described by Gerard de Geer[1] and Ernst Antevs.[2] In this manner, chronological records have been obtained of parts of the retreat of the last ice sheets in Sweden, Finland, and North America. All of these areas were covered and influenced by Pleistocene Glaciation

References

1. Gerard DeGeer, "Geochronologia Suecica Principles," *Suenska Vetenskapsakad,* Handi., Vol. 18, No.6,1940, p.16.
2. Ernst Antevs, "The Recession of the Last Ice Sheet in New England," *American Geog. Soc.,* Research Ser. 11, 1922, P.3. *And:* "Retreat of the Last Ice Sheet in Eastern Canada," *Geol. Survey of Canada,* Mem. 146, 1925, P.9.

Relative Versus Absolute Methods of Dating

Relative dating methods provide information about the succession of fossil assemblages, and archaeological assemblages through time, however it does not tell how old they are or how long they lasted. Geologists and archaeologists must rely on some kind of absolute dating methods to answer these questions.

Some dating methods that geologists and archaeologists rely upon are techniques such as tree ring dating, varve clay dating, radiocarbon, potassium-argon, rubidium-strontium and uranium-lead dating methods. It must be remembered that all these methods have their limitations and never give truly absolute dates, but are often the most reliable that man has been able to discover. The age estimate of 4.6 billion years for the Earth is not an absolute date, but it may be in the ballpark. The Earth may actually be considerably older or younger. Only the Creator of the Earth knows its exact age in earth years and has chosen not to reveal this specific information to Man.

If an archaeological find can be authenticated by history, then this date is considered absolute. For example, the Roman city of Pompeii was destroyed by a volcanic eruption in A.D. 79, when it was completely covered by volcanic ash. Archaeologists know precisely the age of this ancient city in terms of earth years. They are thus able to analyze organic objects within the city and to relate carbon-14 dates to the known historical date.

The relative methods of dating are trial-and-error processes to achieve a means of dating the Earth, plant and animal history, and the duration of time that Man has been on the Earth. Geologists and archaeologists have used these methods, and it was later found that great errors were made. The so called absolute methods of dating have often given a more realistic approach to time; however, they too must be taken with a grain of salt.

The Fossil Method of Dating

The fossil method of dating is based upon the premise that each time unit, such as the Devonian for instance, have index fossils or groups of fossils that are unique to that particular geological age; therefore if similar assemblages of fossils are found elsewhere throughout the Earth, then they could be related in time to the original type section.

Earth scientists establish a "fossil zone," which is a set of beds which contain an index fossil or group of fossils from which the age of the beds can be identified. These zones are gathered into stages, and the stages grouped into series to form a detailed time-stratigraphic division called a "type section." If similar assemblages of fossils and index fossils are found in far-away places, then this sedimentary section is placed in the same relative time scale.

As the science of geology has advanced, it has been discovered that every time unit has unique assemblages of plant and animal life which are often global in distribution. For instance, the Devonian Period in Europe has fossil assemblages similar to those found in North America. The disadvantage with the Fossil dating method is that it is impossible to ascribe Earth years to the different time units. Any estimation of time is guess work, and very relative.

It was not until radiometric methods of dating were discovered that Earth years could be attached to the different time units.

Dating of Sediments

The science of geology is only about 200 years old. The first attempts to date geological time was to classify the rocks of the Earth from the standpoint of age or origin into a two-fold division called the Primary and Secondary rocks. The Primary rocks were the granites, schists, slates, and other crystalline rocks, some of which were thought to represent the original crust of the Earth. The Secondary were the great series of fossiliferous strata resting on the Primary. Later, the units Tertiary and Quaternary were added to comparatively recent, largely unconsolidated sediments.

The term Primary is now replaced by Archean and Proterozoic, the so called "Transition" between Primary and Secondary is largely equivalent to what is now called Paleozoic, and the Secondary is represented by the Mesozoic. The names Tertiary and Quaternary remain. These above mentioned units became known as Eras and Periods. See Figure 1-1.

An era is the largest division of the time scale. It is defined by unusually pronounced and widespread interruptions in sedimentation and by accompanying apparently sudden and great changes in the nature of life. It became obvious that each era represented an enormously long interval of time.

Each era was then subdivided into periods. A period represents a smaller unit of time and is also represented by pronounced and widespread interruptions in sedimentation and by sudden changes in the nature of life. However these changes are less pronounced and are smaller.

Each period is subdivided into epochs and ages. Each epoch represents a smaller time unit depending upon the existence of minor, but important, changes in conditions during the period. An age may overlap several epochs, for example the Age of Reptiles, or the Age of Man.

The *Rjzte of Sedimentation Method* was used at one time to determine geological time. This was based upon the principle of the "Hour Glass," where the rate of fall of sand grains through the tiny aperture of the glass is constant, and the amount of fallen sand at a given instant is directly proportional to the lapse of time since the measurement was begun. In like manner, if the accumulation of sand and other sediments by natural agencies to form stratified rock takes place at a certain constant rate, and if the total amount of sedimentary rocks and the rate of deposition are known, the time represented by the making of the rocks may be roughly computed. Several determinations of the age of the earth on the basis of the thickness of stratified rocks have been undertaken, but they are not very reliable. The conclusions are uncertain because the rates of sedimentation differ greatly for different kinds of sediments, because these rates are not exactly known, and because they are evidently not constant even for rocks of the same composition. To complicate matters more, the measurements of the total thickness of the sedimentary rocks can be inaccurate, and no satisfactory account can be taken of the time represented by interruptions of sedimentation (disconformities and nonconformities). However, in spite of the shortcomings of this method, it did indicate that the Earth was millions of years old.

APPENDIX G

The Three Heavens

The concept of Heaven is entrenched in our literature, our culture and our thinking. Every person has a deep inner desire to go to Heaven, but the question arises, where is Heaven located? What is Heaven like? How do I get there?

The Bible has much to say about Heaven and we are told in Genesis 1:8 that, "*God called the firmament Heaven.*" Is Heaven no greater than the firmament, which is the hydrosphere? Is this the same Heaven mentioned in Genesis 1:1 which says, In the beginning God created the Heavens and the Earth. Could there possibly be more than one Heaven? Paul speaks about being taken up to the Third Heaven for we read in 2 Corinthians 12:2, "*God knows, such a one was caught up to the Third Heaven.*" It becomes evident upon analyzing and comparing the various passages of scripture that the Bible is describing three Heavens (see Figure 1).

The Hebrew word for Heaven is Shomayim. It is a noun that is always in the plural. It is used to describe each of the three Heavens. All three Heavens reflect the Trinity of God. They are in reality One Heaven with three distinct component parts.

The First Heaven

From the vantage point of Man standing on the earth, the first Heaven that one observes is the firmament. Genesis 1:8 says, *"God called the firmament Heaven." We read in Psalm 19:1b, "The firmament shows God's handiwork."* When one observes the beautiful mountains, the sweeping prairies, the vast desert areas, the lush, beautiful vegetation of the tropics, one is beholding what the Bible is referring to as the "First Heaven." It is literally teaming with plant and animal life of all descriptions. It is that portion of our Earth that is able to sustain life. It encompasses the oceans with all its aquatic life, and the biosphere where you and I dwell. Every breath of air that we breath is a gift from the First Heaven. It is a beautiful place that is very much alive.

The Second Heaven

The Second Heaven is the physical universe. The very first verse of the Bible says, *"In the beginning God created the Heavens and the earth"* (Genesis 1:1). From the vantage point of the earth looking out into space, all the heavenly bodies including the sun, moon and stars are included with this Heaven. The psalmist briefly describes this Heaven, *"When I consider thy heavens, the work of your fingers, the moon and the stars that you have ordained, what is man that You are mindful of him,"* (Psalm 8:3). The Second Heaven includes the millions of galaxies, quasars, pulsars, solar systems, spheres of all descriptions and sizes in this vast area called the universe.

The fact that God is present throughout the universe makes it very much alive. The Bible is very clear that God's holy angels are continually commuting back and forth from the Third Heaven to the Earth and always for a specific purpose. It is also possible that God's holy angelic beings are being delegated by God to various parts of the universe for specific purposes. For instance when Jesus was born in Bethlehem 2000 years ago, an angel appeared to the Shepherds announcing the good news that a Savior had been born who is Christ the Lord. This was followed by a great company of the heavenly hosts who were praising God and saying, "*Glory to God in the highest, and on earth peace to men on whom His favor rests.*" (Luke 2: 8—14).

The Third Heaven

The Bible describes the Third Heaven as God's home. Paul tells about an experience of having been caught up into the Third Heaven for we read, "*I know a man in Christ who fourteen years ago was caught up to the THIRD HEAVEN,*" (2 Corinthians 12:2). in the context of this chapter, we realize Paul was literally taken up into the Third Heaven. He was taken to Paradise. This is where the Heavenly Mount Zion is located. This is where our prayers ascend. This is where God the Son, the Lord Jesus Christ is seated at the right hand of God the Father, continually interceding on our behalf. This is the Mission Control centre of the universe. God has complete control over the entire universe and over all creation from the Third Heaven. He knows exactly what is taking place at every place at all times.

The Third Heaven is God's home and is very much alive. The Bible gives many references to the beauty and grandeur of this Heaven. In Psalm 48: 1-3 we read, "*Great is the Lord and most worthy of praise, in the city of our God, his holy mountain. It is beautiful in its loftiness, the joy of the whole earth. Like the utmost heights of Zaphon is Mount Zion, the city of the Great King. God is in her citadels.*" Then we read in Hebrews 12:22-24, "*You have come to Mount Zion, to the heavenly Jerusalem, the city of the living God. You have come to thousands of angels in joyful assembly, to the church of the firstborn, whose names are written in heaven. You have come to God, the judge of all men, to the spirits of righteous men made perfect, to Jesus the mediator of the new covenant and to the sprinkled blood that speaks a better word than the blood of Able."*

The only part of reality that is detectable by our five senses is the physical universe. We as finite human beings are able to see and observe the First and Second Heavens, but we are unable to see or discern the Third Heaven, because it resides within the realm of the invisible. It is within a different frequency or dimension. According to the Bible, reality consists of both the visible and the invisible for we read, *"For by Him (the Lord Jesus Christ) all things were created that are in Heaven and on earth, visible and invisible, whether thrones or rulers or authorities. All things were created by Him and for Him. And He is before all things and in Him all things hold together"* (Colossians 1:16&17, NIV).

The Three Heavens as One

The Third Heaven, where God dwells, is often referred to as the Highest Heaven or the Heaven of Heavens. We read in Nehemiah 9:6, *"You are the Lord. You made the Heavens (second Heaven), even the Highest Heavens, and all their starry host (third heaven), the earth and all things on it, the seas and all that is in them (first heaven), and You give life to everything. The hosts of heaven worship you."* The hosts of Heaven refer to all of God's holy angelic beings and to all human beings who have and will receive Jesus Christ as their personal Savior and Lord. Thus, we see that the First Heaven includes the oceans as well as the earth with its great variety of life. It becomes apparent that the First and Third Heavens are very much alive. Is it possible that the Second Heaven may also be very much alive? The omnipresence of the Triune God throughout the entire universe makes it very much alive. It is also highly possible that God's holy angels commute back and forth from the Third Heaven to various parts of the universe. We can safely say that all three Heavens are very much alive.

The Bible acknowledges God as the sole owner of the three Heavens for we read in Deuteronomy 10:14, *"To the Lord your God belong the heavens (Second Heaven), the highest heaven (Third Heaven), the earth and everything in it (First Heaven)."* God has total ownership of His creation by the mere fact that He is the Creator of all things. The Bible says, *"For every animal of the forest is mine, and the cattle on a thousand hills. I know every bird in the mountains and the creatures of the field are Mine. If I were hungry I would not tell you, for the world is Mine, and all that is in it"* (Psalm 50:10-11 NIV). In other words, He owns every species and variety of animal and plant life on the earth. He has placed Man on the earth to look after and to be a good steward of all that He has made for we read, *"Let us make man in our image, in our likeness, and let them rule over the fish of the sea and the birds of the air, over the livestock, over all the creatures that move along the ground."* (Genesis 1:26 NIV)

We may stand in awe at the wonders, beauty, and magnificence of God's creation as revealed in the First and Second Heavens. However, this is only a glimpse of a far surpassing beauty, magnificence, vastness, glory and awesomeness of the Third Heaven which is God's home and will also be our future home. If the Third Heaven appears great and glorious, how much greater, more glorious, beautiful, majestic and awesome must God be. Even reason and logic say to us that the Creator must always be greater than what He has created for we read, *"The Lord is high above all nations and His glory is above the Heavens"* (Psalm 113:4).

Where is Heaven Located?

Dr. Irwin Moon, producer of the Moody Institute of Science films, had the following interview about Heaven with a famous physicist who had won the Nobel Prize for his achievement in the "Porosity of Matter." The conversation is as follows:

Dr. Moon: Do you believe in God?

Scientist: Oh yes, in fact all scientists I know believe in God. The closer you get to the basic construction of matter, the more you know there has to be a God. But don't get me wrong, I don't believe in God the way you do.

Dr. Moon: What is the difference?

Scientist: Let me ask you a question. Where is heaven located?

Dr. Moon: We used to say "up", but now that we know the world is round, we say it is `out' instead of `up'.

Scientist: How far is out?

Dr. Moon: I don't know?

Scientist: Is Abel in heaven?

Dr. Moon: Yes, Abel is in heaven.

Scientist: How did he get there?

Dr. Moon: I don't know.

Scientist: If heaven is located just beyond the range of my telescope and Abel has been travelling at the speed of light for 6,000 years, he is only a tiny portion of the distance that I have seen with my telescope. So, assuming that heaven is just beyond the range of my telescope, he has literally thousands of years yet to go before he reaches heaven.

Dr. Moon: Doctor, you have received the Nobel prize for your work in physics. You have done more than any other person to popularize the idea of the porosity of matter. Now, if your research is true, is this wall mostly space?

Scientist: yes, it's about as porous as a breath of fresh air.

Dr. Moon: If this wall is porous and this chair is porous, why can't I push the chair through the wall the same way I can push my fingers in between one another?

Scientist: I don't know why you can't push the chair through the wall. I have tried it and it won't go through. But this I know, it is not because there is a collision of the solid particles. we assume that between the solid particles there is an electrical flux operating on opposing frequencies. To illustrate this, take two horseshoe magnets and try pushing them together, like poles against like poles. You will discover that there is a strong electrical force that keeps you from doing it. This is what the scientist is saying about opposing frequencies.

Dr. Moon: If your theory is true, would it be possible then for two earth's to occupy the same space at the same time and neither be conscious of the other's existence if they were perfectly synchronized by frequency so that there are no collisions?

Scientist: (after thinking a moment): Yes, not only two, but hundred's of thousands of earth's could occupy the very same space.

Dr. Moon: I think I have learned something very valuable from this conversation. Just this morning I was reading Ephesians 2:6, which says, "*We are seated in heavenly places in Christ Jesus.*" To get to Heaven I may not have to move an inch. All I have to do is to change to a different frequency. [1]According to the Bible the Third Heaven is closer than we realize. There is a thin veil that separates you and I from the Third Heaven. As an example, when Stephen was stoned as a martyr, the Bible reports, "*But Stephen, full of the Holy Spirit, looked up to heaven and saw the glory of*

God, and Jesus standing at the right hand of God. `Look' he said, `I see Heaven open and the Son of Man standing at the right hand of God." (Acts 7:55-56). Stephen was given a glimpse into the Third Heaven, or in other words into the throne room of the universe just prior to his death. This makes us aware that the Third Heaven is near at all times.

References

1. Downing James, *"Does God Care About You"*, The Navigators Log, Oct. 1971, Colorado Springs
2. All scripture references are from the New International Version or the Revised King James version of the Bible.